To Linh, Théo, Thomas and Enzo
You are the reasons why I wrote this book

"Leaders are merchants of hope"

Napoléon Bonaparte

WHY SHOULD THEY CARE?

5-STEP METHOD TO IGNITE YOUR TEAM ENGAGEMENT AND MOTIVATION

DAVID SERENE

About the Author

David Serene is veterinarian graduated at Veterinary school in France. He worked for 15 years in the Animal Pharmaceutical industries in leadership positions in Vietnam, Thailand and South Africa. He founded his own company in Vietnam and Thailand marketing new technologies for Animal nutrition. In 2011, David Serene created TOTEM Management Consulting, a consulting firm in Hong Kong specialized in leadership and performance management.

David Serene made many consultations in South East Asia for local companies and multinationals across many industries among them Total, Vétoquinol, Servier, Cargill, Horizon Software, CPIT, etc…

David Serene is driven by a deep and long admiration for historical leaders who got the courage to share their vision sometimes against the forces of their time and who accomplished miracles through discipline and dedication.

David Serene has always been passionate about leadership and wanted to share his view on the subject through this book with a very practical approach.

There is a general consensus that most employees do not enjoy their work. They are working just for the payroll, by necessity. They show up in the morning without any sense of commitment. They see their job as boring and consider their bosses as an opponent who will make their life difficult and that they need to fight. Studies show that only one-third of workers are engaged in their work. The other two-thirds are either neutral or actively disengaged.

There is a large pit today between companies' leaders and their team. Management has a very bad press but they are paying for the wrong message that they have been communicating for years. Managers are asking workers to dedicate a third of their time in exchange for a salary and job security. But the reality is that salary today is under pressure and long-term employment does not exist anymore.

At the opposite, gaining employees support and engagement is more critical than ever for managers. The real point of competitiveness of every organization is their ability to get their employees committed to what they are doing. If you compare companies in the same industry, they can copy each other in many areas. They develop similar strategies, steal employees from each other, and apply similar processes. The only dimension that is difficult to replicate and that will make a difference, in the long run, will be the amount of energy and dedication that their employees will show in executing their job.

We should see employees going to the office every morning full of energy and committing to the mission they have been assigned. They should be excited by the project they are participating too and believe that their daily effort can make a difference. They should thrive to reach the short, medium and long-term ambitions that they define with their peers. They should feel part of a community who share the same values and practices and enjoy working together. Finally, they should feel successful. Their success at work should enable them to be recognized as useful and important. But we are still far from this idealistic world.

How can we reconcile these 2 conflicting worlds? How is it possible that so much energy is misused and generates so much opposition, disappointment, and frustration when it should actually contribute to making the world more efficient and happier place?

It is for sure a problem of leadership. We need to find a common center of interest for all parties. We already know that it cannot be money for which the interest could be divergent, especially if the shareholders are short-term orientated. Leaders (and I wrote it plural as we will see later than it is never a one-man job) need to find motives for workers to care. We will see in this book that every individual has some drivers. It is the leaders' job to find them and leverage them. These drivers need to be sincere and sustainable if the leaders want to stay credible in the long run. It is about giving a meaning to others' job.

So what do leaders do wrong? How is it possible that we missed out the point that much? There are hundreds of books on leadership. Every company organizes regular seminars and training on leadership for their managers. I went through such training when I was working in the pharmaceutical industry. They often present some aspects of the leadership but they rarely present an exhaustive approach of leadership.

Moreover, with the development of teleworking, the context is changing. Employees get more independence but interactions between employees with their colleagues and their bosses get fewer. There are more written communication and less informal discussions. Leaders need to adjust their style to this new environment if they do not want to lose grasp on their team.

The intuitive leadership style that was working in an office before may be challenged by the new working norms. Leaders need to adjust their leadership approach to take into account the teleworking situation. Employees practices, expectations are changing and leaders must adapt.

For leadership to be effective, it is critical to connect the 5 keystones that I present in this book. If you miss one step, your colleagues will immediately note the inconsistency and doubt the whole process.

Leaders' success is measured through their ability to engage effectively their colleagues into actions. That requires a minimum understanding of the mechanisms of leadership that they did neither learn at school or in the previous jobs.

Leadership is the ability to enlist the aid and support of others in the accomplishment of a common task. This book aims at presenting to readers a methodology that I developed and experienced for the past 20 years in the executive positions in Europe, Asia, and Africa.

The value behind leadership relies on three essential benefits that are team engagement, stakeholders' alignment and job clarifications.

Leadership is not limited to large or small organizations but should cover companies with any sizes. Leadership does not concern only top managers but should be developed at every level of the organization.

This book will enable readers to cover all the dimensions of leadership. We will go through the 5 dimensions of leadership, and explain why these 5 dimensions are critical for ensuring engagement, alignment and clarifications and how you can exercise them in your daily life and work.

This book could interest anybody who is managing subordinates and would like to obtain more support from their team. You want to maximize your impact on your organization by leveraging employees' engagement and alignment; engagement will trigger more care, higher energy, and dedication. Alignment will bring about better organization efficiency and smoother collaboration between employees and clarifications will build a secure and effective working environment.

I chose the corporate world to illustrate the leadership methodology. But as you go through the book, you will realize that similar guiding principles apply the same way to our private sphere. As an autonomous adult and as parents, leadership is a key skill that we need to focus on to reach the balance we are all looking for.

My main intention in working this book is to convince readers that leadership is not for some happy few but it is a pivotal question in our society. There is one central question that we should all want to answer;

WHY SHOULD OTHERS CARE?

Copyright © 2019 by David Serene

All rights reserved. No part(s) of this book may be reproduced, distributed or transmitted in any form, or by any means, or stored in a database or retrieval systems without prior expressed written permission of the author of this book.

Book Interior Designed by

Hmdgfx

Table of Contents

1 We are all leaders 1
    1.1 Leadership is to be learned 1
    1.2 Everybody is a leader 2
    1.3 Leader or Manager 3

2. Why every Organization needs Leadership? 8
    2.1. Engagement 9
    2.2. Alignment 16
    2.3. Clarifications 17

3. Why are we missing our point? 19
    3.1. The world is driven by self-interest 21
    3.2. Leadership starts with us 23
    3.3. It not urgent but important 25

4. Leaders are Associated to a Vision 27
    4.1 Leaders exist through their vision 27
    4.2 How do vision differ from mission 30
    4.3 The traps to avoid 34
    4.4 The cascade of vision 37
    4.5 The butterfly effect 39
    4.6. The importance of the strategy 41

5. How leaders shape team culture? 46
    5.1 What is the corporate culture? 46
    5.2 Reference behaviors 49
    5.3 The contribution of legends 52
    5.4 How do leaders build / reinforce / change corporate culture?
    53

5.5 What is a good culture? *58*

6. The importance of execution 61

6.1 Our leadership architecture *61*
6.2 The theory of motivation *63*
6.3 We get only what we measure *67*
6.4 The road map *69*
6.5 The Behavioral performance *80*
6.6 How to obtain employees buy-in into the performance system? 83
6.7 The importance of coaching 88
6.8 The benefits behind the Performance Management System 90

CONCLUSION **97**

I

We are all leaders

1.1 Leadership is to be learnt

One of the myths about leadership is that it is determined by distinctive dispositional characteristics present at birth (e.g., extraversion, intelligence, ingenuity, charisma). However, according to Forsyth (2009,), there is evidence to show that leadership also develops through hard work and careful observation. Thus, effective leadership can result from nature (i.e., innate talents) as well as nurture (i.e., acquired skills). Through this book, we will explain the mechanisms that trigger a positive response from the audience we are targeting.

I cannot guarantee that every reader will become an outstanding leader by reading this book but I am guaranteeing to provide readers a method to improve their leadership skills. The method that I am presenting in the following pages is centered around five themes; MISSION, VISION, STRATEGY, CULTURE, and PERFORMANCE

These five pillars are the areas of expertise of the leaders. We will describe more in details in the following pages each of these elements. For each of them, the leader is responsible for elaborating the content and ensures a good understanding of all his team members through an efficient and frequent communication.

1.2 Everybody is a leader

Another misconception that we need to underline at this stage of the document is the idea that there is only one leader per organization. I am actually promoting that every employee has a leadership role.

First, whatever position we have in our organization, we are a relay in the transmission of our company vision and culture, either to our subordinates, our peers or the new employees. To be efficient in relaying this information, it is important to understand its nature and how it is articulating. The better we will understand the goal and mechanisms of leadership and the more efficient we will be to relay the message around us.

Moreover, department managers have another leadership responsibility. The logic of engagement, alignment, and clarifications that apply to the organization level will apply the same way to each department. Managers can contribute by adding their own layer.

Indeed, financial, manufacturing or marketing department managers can develop their own vision of how do they see the success of their department. It is their job to clarify what they expect precisely from their team to make this success possible. The department vision cannot come in opposition to the CEO's vision but it should come in addition. Indeed, every employee is participating to as many projects as the number of the team he belongs to.

I strongly believe that educating all employees about leadership mechanism should be a general requirement for all employees, whether they are managers, team leaders or only a relay in the organization. By better understanding the mechanisms of leadership and therefore the role and contribution of their hierarchical superiors, it will facilitate understanding and alignment within teams.

Parents as well need to seriously work on their leadership. Parenting is certainly the most important mission that we have been assigned to. It naturally positions us as a leader in the eyes of children who are looking at us for answers. Isn't parenting about embodying for them an attractive vision of what could be their future, defining clear values and behaviors and accompanying them through the achievement and failure or any other feedback on their performance that life is giving them.

1.3 Leader or Manager

There is a general blur about the differences between management and leadership. We often use both qualifications for each other's, and we do not see clearly the functions of each. There are actually 3 distinct roles in each organization

- Experts who know how to perform a task
- Managers who decide what to do and when to do it
- Leaders who explain why we are doing it

Management is about organizing the delivery. Management is about WHAT to do and WHEN to do it. Management is the science to ensure that each train arrives on time.

An expert will then do the job. Experts are the best at doing the job. They know HOW to do it to deliver the WHAT and WHEN that manager requires.

Both management and expertise is about repetition, optimization, and effectiveness. Both hate disruption, changes, and surprises. Management defines standards and experts deliver them. When the processes are well established and expectations do not change, management and expertise are sufficient to run a company. We do not need leaders. And, regrettably, this is what is happening in many organizations.

But when adaptations and changes are required, the exercise requires a different set of skills. It requires leadership in order to

- Explain why the change is required and encourage managers and experts to leave their comfort zone

- Minimize frictions in the team when changes are applied

- Give sufficient clarifications on the new expectations

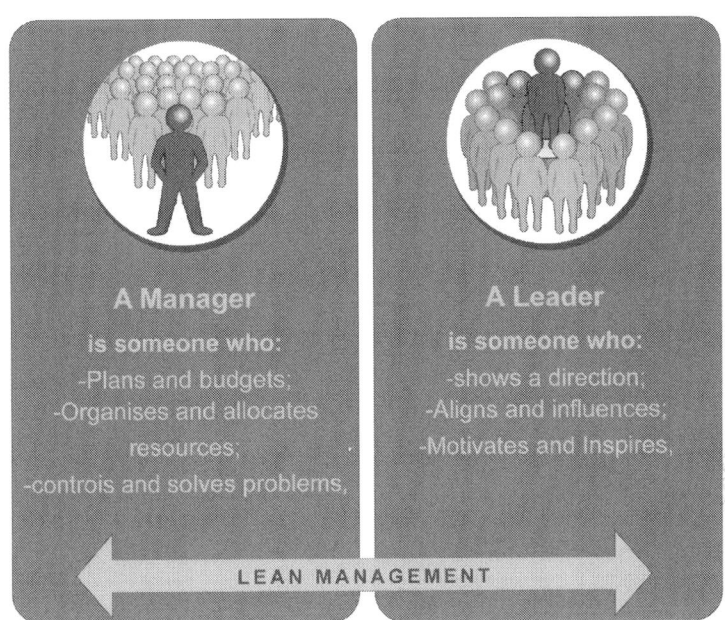

"Managers work in the system while leaders work on the system"

The most efficient tool of leaders is the question WHY. It is the most powerful question. It obliges to go deeply into understanding motives. It helps to shake the status quo. The answer to this question helps to understand the mechanism behind the scenes in order then to leverage them to ensure sustainable motivation and engagement. To get full alignment and support in a team, they must agree on the WHY first. Once they get there, the what, when and how will become much easier to agree on.

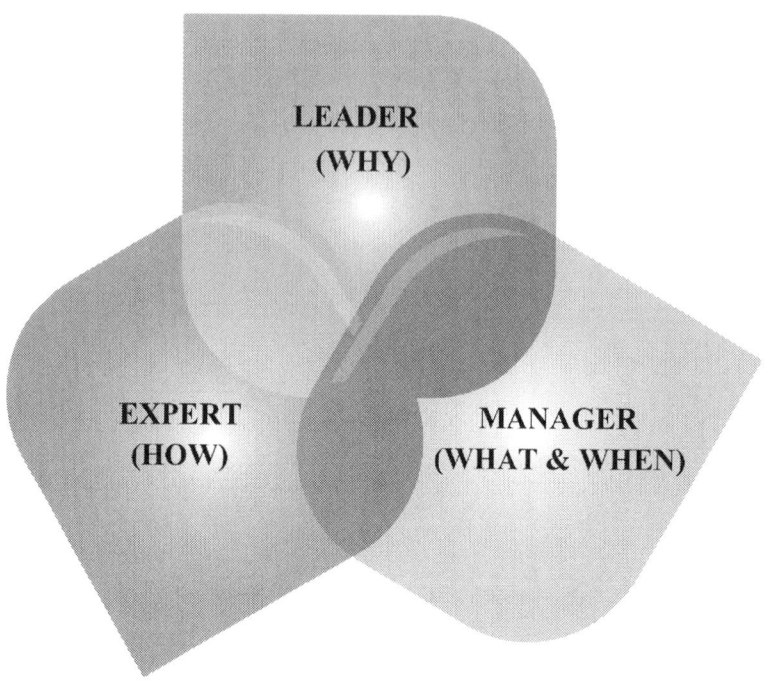

We are often ourselves a mix of these 3 functions in our organization; expert, manager, and leader at the same time. The lower we are in the organization, the more predominant is the expertise dimension and the lower is the leadership side. The higher we climb in an organization and the more critical management and leadership dimensions are.

In a very large organization, some CEO's role is exclusively about leadership with a very little contribution to execution.

Expertise is learned at schools. Young graduates join the corporate world with very little or no knowledge about management and leadership and they are expected to learn management and leadership through experience.

As a child, we are encouraged to ask questions, to be curious about life, and to find out your inner drivers. However, as we grow into an adult our curiosity diminishes, we stop asking questions, stop challenging, and become more concerned with fitting in than questioning certain things in life. As we grow and develop, our fears, doubts, and worries grow too, the questions stop.

I encourage being curious again and finding the WHY behind everything. You may destabilize your colleagues and your managers by always searching the motives. You need to explain to them smoothly the reasons behind your interrogations and they may understand and contribute to your thinking which in return will participate to the team alignment.

- Why should I contribute to this project?
- Why should I make a consensus with my teammate?
- Why should I change my behaviors to suit the team?
- Why do I like my job?
- Why should we grow our business?

And the leader is the person who will give you satisfying answers to these questions. The leader will give the reasons why you should do it. He will underline convincingly what there is for you and what it would mean for you to achieve these missions. He will detail precisely what is expected from you and he will explain it so clearly that it will look easy to achieve. A good leader will explain WHY it is in your interest to do it.

2.

Why every Organization needs Leadership?

We always believe that dedication and engagement is a given in a company. From the first day collaborators join the company, they would do everything they can to make the company successful. And it happens sometimes. We all know or hear about companies where it is fun to work. Employees enjoyed what they are doing. They believe that they are contributing to something useful. They clearly understand their role and the roles of their colleagues. They are helping each other. They have an honest and constructive relationship with their boss who gives them regular feedback on their development and progress. They are feeling successful. They speak well about their company and indeed thrive at achieving higher output. Such a company exists and we should all aim at creating such an environment.

There could be many reasons to explain such 'happy' atmosphere, but the main driver is the leading architecture.

The reason why I call it leadership architecture is because it is designed as we design a house, starting by the lay out before building up the walls and roofs. The component of leadership architecture that we will cover in this book is embedded in the company foundation. They are part of the organization genes and culture. It does not depend on one person but is now part of the organization itself. It may have started from an individual who initiated the elaboration of this leadership architecture. With time, it is transmitted through all the organization and the next generation.

Leadership aims at three essential characteristics that we find in all the successful teams; ENGAGEMENT, ALIGNMENT and CLARIFICATIONS

2.1. Engagement

For outstanding results, we need to get our colleagues willing and committed. We need to get them excited about what they are doing and what they are trying to achieve. For leaders, it is a tough sell. Employees must have good reasons for fighting for their company's success. The leaders must understand employees motive and redirect their ambition and energy towards a common goal that they will all find worthy and exciting. If leaders can get employees to contribute, they will start achieving outstanding results.

It is possible to measure the level of engagement through surveys. You can find on the net several questionnaires developed by specialized companies.

I am using myself a questionnaire designed by Gallup. The participants need to grade 12 questions from 1 to 10 (1 being the lowest score).

- I know what is expected of me at work
- I feel successful at what I am doing at work
- In the last seven days, I have received recognition or praise for doing good work
- My supervisor, or someone at work, seems to care about me as a person
- There is someone at work who encourages my development
- At work, my opinions seem to count
- The mission or purpose of my company makes me feel my job is important
- My fellow employees are committed to doing quality work
- I have best friends at work
- In the last six months, someone at work talked to me about my progress
- This last year, I have had opportunities at work to learn and grow
- I am proud to say that I work for my company

The answers enable to classify employees into 3 categories; Engaged, Not Engaged and Actively Disengaged.

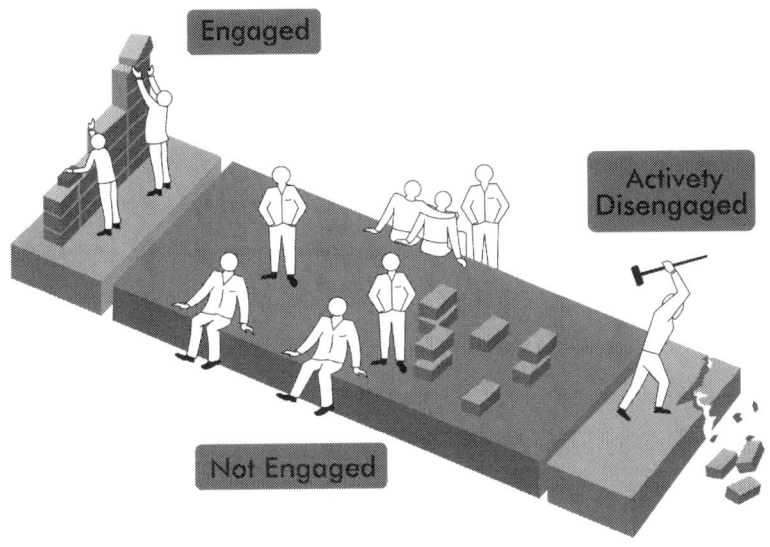

Engaged Employees -" Engaged employees work with passion and feel a profound connection to their company. They drive innovation and move the organization forward."

Not Engaged Employees -" Not engaged employees are essentially 'checked out.' They're sleepwalking through their workday, putting time — but not energy or passion — into their work."

Actively Disengaged Employees - "Actively disengaged employees aren't just unhappy at work; they're busy acting out their unhappiness. Every day, these workers undermine what their engaged coworkers accomplish."

When employees are engaged, they adopt the purpose, vision, values of the organization they work for. They become passionate contributors, innovating problem solvers, and stunning colleagues. They exemplify the rule of the 3 S. They Stay, Strive and Speak; they Stay long in an organization, they Strive to achieve their goals and contribute to the team's effort and they Speak positively about their job to their colleagues and friends.

Employees who are "not engaged" are those who have problems with the way things work. But inherently they aren't bad people. With the right strategies and level of involvement from leaders, "not engaged" employees can be turned into "engaged" employees

The biggest threat that is posed to organizations is the third category of employees, those who are "actively disengaged."

"Actively disengaged" employees tend to hold a grudge toward the company. They go out of their way to disrupt operations or can even act out subconsciously. It's the veteran employee who lost the promotion to the new guy; it's the employee who justifies using the company card for a personal purchase because she or he feels undervalued.

The "actively disengaged" employees are a huge cost to the company. It is extremely crucial for organizations to understand who these employees are as they actually set out to damage businesses. Not only do such employees show their resentment through being unproductive, but they also indulge in unprofessional behaviors and demotivate those around them. Their activities plague companies and drag down productivity that can damage businesses.

Recent studies made on the US workforce underlined surprising results.

Of the 100 million people in the U.S. workforce...

- Only 30 percent of U.S. workers are engaged and inspired at work.
- 20 percent of U.S. workers are actively disengaged.
- 50 percent of U.S. workers are present, but not engaged or inspired within their workplace.

Employee engagement is at its highest level since Gallup first began measuring the performance indicator in 2000. As Gallup has reported, public perceptions of the economy and job market are increasingly positive following improved GDP growth and lower unemployment. Workers' improved engagement levels could be a reflection of the country's improved economic conditions. The engagement began to drop in 2008 during the financial collapse and continued to fall in 2009, not showing any signs of improvement until 2011, and then reaching its current peak in 2014.

Employee engagement initiatives have also become more commonplace since Gallup first introduced its Q12 employee engagement survey in the late 1990s, with nearly 30 million workers being assessed on the instrument along with managerial training. Many organizations increasingly assess their managers on engagement metrics and expect them to maintain employees' engagement levels. Employee engagement levels might be rising to some degrees because managers increasingly see engaging employees as a natural part of their duties. Managers are giving engagement more attention than they have in the past, potentially leading to higher engagement percentages.

When we look outside the US, the level of engagement is dropping to only 13%, according to Gallup's new 142-country study on the State of the Global Workplace. In other words, about one in eight workers -- roughly 180 million employees in the countries studied -- are psychologically committed to their jobs and likely to be making positive contributions to their organizations. The other 1.2 billion employees are either "not engaged" or "actively disengaged".

Employee Engagement Repartition, by Zone

	Engaged	Not Engaged	Actively Disengaged
United States and Canada	29%	54%	18%
Australia and New Zealand	24%	60%	16%
Latin America	21%	60%	19%
Western Europe	14%	66%	20%
Southeast Asia	12%	73%	14%
Central and Eastern Europe	11%	63%	26%
Middle East and North Africa	10%	55%	35%
South Asia	10%	61%	29%
Sub-Saharan Africa	10%	57%	33%
East Asia	6%	68%	26%

GALLUP 2011-2012

When we monitor the level of engagement of the same employee over the years, we notice that employees get fully engaged when they start a new job or a new mission but they often get dis-engaged over time when disillusion, frustration and routine kick in. The level of engagement starts high as their managers often did a good job in 'selling' the mission underlining benefits and exciting goals. But, the difficulties of daily operations bring up disappointment and managers are often too busy to notice it and even more to re-engage employees. If routine gets engagement to fade, leaders should turn it into 'project' mode. The 'project' mode will oblige the leader to make a special effort in defining the project goals, the role of each participant, the collaborative behaviors. All employees should jump from 'project' to 'project' to maintain a high level of engagement. It may be difficult to create projects when you lead an accounting or a manufacturing department, but it is not impossible.

2.2. Alignment

In every organization, there are points of frictions between department and employees because of different agendas and personalities. These frictions are natural and can be healthy to a certain point and as long as the mood stays constructive.

But leaders must find a way to minimize these frictions to be sure that all the energy is used constructively to perform. Leaders must ensure that employees share the same agenda, same working rules in order to maximize team collaboration in the organization and promote constructive communication together with mutual help.

Team alignment is not a natural process. If you form a team, there is little chance that all participants will have similar goals and motives. We often try to force alignment by authority and threats. We may get everybody in the rank but we will never get him or her energized if they are not convinced and it will require too much energy from the manager to maintain the rank.

Rather than pushing, it is much more efficient and sustainable to create an aspiration that will make all team members excited by the idea to succeed as a team. This aspiration is leadership and we will detail in the following pages the mechanisms that leaders will use to align the team.

2.3. Clarifications

To organize their work efficiently, we all need to get visibility on the coming days and months. We need to have a clear understanding of our roles, our contribution, and our interactions with others, our targets and our resources. When this is possible, we can plan our tasks efficiently. We will have the liberty to organize our time and allocate our energy the way we believe is right. This gives us a full ownership of our projects and the results obtained. When the results are positive, it triggers pride and recognition for a work that we managed autonomously.

But the problem is that we are facing a constantly changing environment and that we need to adapt to keep on serving the request of our internal and external customers. The leader must actually be the interface between the outside and the inside to manage change. If leader accepts all required changes, he will put his team under a lot of pressure and do not give them the possibility to organize themselves sufficiently. If the leader refuses any changes, the team will lose competitiveness. Therefore, the leader has the difficult task to decide what changes are acceptable for survival and which ones are not (for the sake of optimization). The leader must focus on offering maximal predictability to his team so that they can get the right autonomy and visibility to organize themselves in an efficient way.

The testimonial below is a summary of comments that I often hear when I am visiting companies on the field. These lines underline that there is still a huge room for improvement to move from disengaged organizations to engaged teams.

"In my job, I face constant changes. Every time I am comfortable with the way we are operating; our boss comes with new changes. When a new situation arises, I do not clearly know who in our organization has to handle it. Anyway, there is not a precise and specific measurement of my contribution. I believe that I am doing my job correctly, but I am not sure our boss sees it the same way. I do not clearly know what the other departments of our company are doing. I have little interactions with them except when they are sending us emails to complain about something. The other employees do not really care about their job and I am often negatively impacted by their lack of commitment. Our boss comes to see me only to remind the targets and numbers that I have to deliver. Every year, he comes with higher numbers without any rationale behind the increase except that we need to gain market share from competitors. They are asking us to work harder every year and our salary is not increased accordingly. I am working in my company for many years already and I am now bored. As soon as I found an opportunity, I will try to move to another company."

Does that sound familiar?

3.
Why are we missing our point?

I have been wondering for years why it is so difficult to engage colleagues. I met managers who believed that such opposition between employees and management is their fate. They think that the corporate world is by essence a world of opposition, exploitation where we must show muscles so that winners can walk on the losers' bodies.

I must say that I had my periods of doubt when I was wondering whether I was not too idealistic, whether my vision of the world that I present in the following pages is not too naïve and whether ultimately the 'bad' would not always win over the 'nice guy'. But I refuse to believe so. I still believe in people and dream. I strongly believe that with the right amount of dedication, effort and time, it can work, and we can make the world a better place.

My analysis of the current leadership approach in most of the organization is that we are reproducing patterns and following recipes that we have been told for decades. We are posting a vision on our website and hanging values on our walls because we have been told so. But we rarely question the meaning and rationale behind these technics. Leadership, vision, culture, values are nice words. It looks professional to refer to it in every company profile, but it seldom means anything. Leaders are managers that have been promoted and keep doing their management work but with a higher stake. I am amazed every time that a company manager explains to me what leadership for him is. It used nice words and concept but most of the time it is empty. It does not refer to anything tangible and practical in the daily life of employees' operation. And remember, if it does not impact other's lives, it is not leadership.

Before going through the architecture that I propose, I have been thinking what will be the obstacles that prevent managers to be efficient at leading. It is not a lack of education or intelligence. There are plenty of smart managers around us who went through many trainings on the subject. I believe that they have good intention and are really trying hard to engage their colleagues. But the obstacles are somewhere else.

What are we doing wrong today to prevent leadership to be efficient?

I want to start spending time on the three most damageable misconceptions in the whole corporate world.

3.1. The world is driven by self-interest

We have all been told thousand times that we must place the company interest above ours. We expect that employees will work hard to make the company successful first because they are paid for it and second because they understand their long-term interest.

It does not work this way and I believe it is critical to confess that everything that we do is dictated by our self-interest. Napoleon said, "the world is driven by fear and self-interest". Leaders must accept this element of human psychology. It is not because employees receive a salary and show up at work every morning that you can expect them to fight for the company. Fear of losing what they already have will make them deliver what is required, but only what is required. If you want your team to become proactive, to take initiatives, manage risks and thrive at exceeding what is expected to make the organization better, leaders need to give them a good motive. 'Please' may not be sufficient.

22 | Why Should They Care?

It is not that employees do not want to contribute, it is just that they must get something out of it, they must benefit from the additional efforts they are making.

Money is one of the ways to trigger personal interest, but we will see later that it is not the most efficient. We have hundreds of examples of religious or sportsmen who are realizing extraordinary achievement for little or no money at all. They show a high level of commitment aiming at what they consider the valuable cause. It is important to understand what drives them to re-apply similar context to the corporate world. And it is the responsibility of the leaders to create such a framework. I often shock managers when I say that it is leaders 'duties' to create a context where employees will want to contribute. It is actually leaders' most important job. We all have an inner potential energy that demands to be used. Every employee, whatever the level in the organization gets such energy ready to be leveraged. Leaders may not know how to use it. Those who find the way will transform a team of 'participants' into a team of 'competitors'.

We all tend to blame others first. If our team is not sufficiently motivated or engaged, it is always because of them. We find reasons to explain their lack of commitment. But we rarely, very rarely, actually never call it a lack of leadership skill from the manager. I said that before concluding that team members are not up to the job, think twice about the efforts you did as a leader to leverage their self-interest. Why should they care? What are the reasons you gave them to overperform? It would be faster, cheaper, less tiresome and more efficient for you to become a better leader than using fear to negotiate more output from them.

But it is certainly not by reminding relentlessly that budget is important and must be achieved. Just between us, who cares about the budget....?

3.2. Leadership starts with us

Before starting speaking about leadership, we must agree on the qualification of leaders. Who are the leaders? Who is exercising leadership? Who should be interested in becoming a better leader? We all have a tendency to believe that the leader is the individual or the group of individuals at the top of the organization, the persons that everybody refers to by 'they'.

When I was working in the pharmaceutical industry, I was disappointed to hear my peer's managers answering to their workers; "I cannot do anything about it, it is 'their' decision". It is actually a way to avoid responsibility. It is always easier to blame others and not face a difficult situation.

We should actually feel responsible. Leadership starts with us. Let us not wait for our superiors to change. Most of the points that I described in the 5-step method do not require the validation from the top management to be developed and implemented.

I love this quote about leadership;

"If your actions inspire others to dream more, learn more, do more and become more, you are a leader"

Are you passionate about others? Are you influencing your friends, your colleagues, your children or others to do more?

Actually, we are all leaders.

The question is not whether you are good at that or whether you like or want it. The question is whether you regularly find yourself in such a situation and how you handle it.

It may be a small change at your level but it could appear big for the people you are helping. And if you are lucky and others see it the same way as you, things could really change. If you believe that you are only a paw in the game 'THEY' play, there is no point in reading the following pages. If you believe that you have a role to play to dream more, learn more, do more and become more, I believe that the coming pages can help you to do so.

3.3. It not urgent but important

S.Covey said that urgency creates a sense of importance. I encourage you all to read his book "First things first" where he explained how we all tend to become addicted to urgency.

S.Covey wrote "Some of us get so used to the adrenaline rush of handling crises that we become dependent on it for a sense of excitement and energy. How does urgency feel? Stressful? Pressured? Tense? Exhausting? Sure. But let's be honest. It's also sometimes exhilarating. We feel useful. We feel successful. We feel validated. And we get good at it..... People expect us to be busy, overworked. It's become a status symbol in our society – if we are busy, we are important. If we are not busy, we are almost embarrassed to admit it. Business is where we get our security. It's validating, popular, and pleasing. It's also a good excuse for not dealing with the first things in our lives…Many important things that contribute to our overall objectives and give richness and meaning to life don't tend to act upon us or press us. Because they're not "urgent", they are things that we must act upon."

Building a proper leadership architecture in our organization to provide constructive motives to our team members is never an urgent matter but still critically important. My experience at consulting makes me realized how leadership issues are never clearly identified and timely handled. If you expect to start working on your leadership architecture the day you get some free time, you will never get there. They are always 'nice projects' to be discussed later. But let us face reality…one day, you will need to work on it.

Today could be the moment to start strengthening your leadership skills...or at least to write it on your agenda at a specific date.

4.

Leaders are Associated to a Vision

4.1 Leaders exist through their vision

The history is full of memorable leaders that are all remembered for what they intended to achieve. That vision is their main trademark. Gandhi, Martin Luther King, and Ho Chi Minh stood out of the crowd when they spoke out their vision of the changes they want to bring to their world. It is first the inspiration and promises from their vision that brought them unconditional followers.

"If you are working on something exciting that you really care about, you don't have to be pushed. The vision pulls you." ~ Steve Jobs

The main contribution of a leader to the team is to propose a project that is attractive enough for participants to join. We call this project "a vision". It is a precise and clear description of an ambition that;

- Everybody would be proud to achieve
- Everybody can contribute to
- Realization is visible

People want to be part of something big. They want to work for leaders who give their lives meaning and it is up to the leaders to engage them through the definition of an exciting vision.

The vision is actually an ambition. It is an appealing description of a future state. It does give a common purpose to stakeholders and it must result in emotional engagement. A vision is a visualization of success. It can be the ultimate goal "Achieving 10 million USD of sales on a year" or it can be an illustration of the success of "Get our customers to thank us for our beauty advice". It does not necessarily have to be measurable; it can be only behaviors to encourage from another stakeholder that employees would keep in mind daily when they are at work.

Examples of powerful vision:

- Air Asia - "Get everyone to fly"
- Microsoft - "A computer on every desk and in every home"
- Ford Motor Company (the early 1900's) - "Ford will democratize the automobile"

- Sony (the early 1950's) - "Become the company most known for promoting the quality image of Japanese products"
- Boeing (1950) - "Bring the world into the jet age"
- Pepsi - "Beat Coke"
- Walt Disney Attractions Park - "Get our visitors to exit our park with a larger smile than when they get in"
- Danone - "Get a Danone branded product into every fridge of the world"

We often associate the adjective visionary to leaders. It is not that they see the future through a crystal ball. Who can judge anyway whether their vision of the future will realize or not at the moment they formulate it? Who knew for sure that Apple would become such a success when Steve Jobs define his vision of his future? At that time, what made an impact was not to be sure it will realize or not but it was that Steve Jobs was constantly mentioning to it.

1. He was referring to his vision to justify everything the company was doing. The vision was the main motive on the company agenda.
2. He had a very clear vision. His expectations were clearly defined and he gave many details about it.

Naturally, the vision has to be a nice story, realistic and ambitious enough, underlining successes that all participants would be the pride of. It has to be sincere. It would be difficult to be convincing on the importance of your motives without sufficient authenticity. Our team members will sense it if we do not fully believe in what we are advocating. Vision must be dictating by our heart more than our brain. It is about who we are and what we deeply believe in and it has to speak to our colleagues' hearts as well, mostly about their need for pride.

The second particularity of visionary leader is the number of details they give to illustrate their vision. It is not about foreseeing the future. It is about choosing what they want to 'see'. They have a very clear understanding of what is required to become successful and they pay a high level of importance to define their expectations in details. They want to give very clear indications to their colleagues. Clarification is an important driver of visionary leaders.

It may require some practicing before being able to develop and communicate an impactful vision.

You need to let your story mature. You may adjust it according to your audience to ensure that it will resonate for them. And if you keep it at the center of your agenda with a high level of details, you will definitively start impacting your colleagues.

4.2 How do vision differ from mission

The first act of leadership is to define the nature of our business. We call that definition the corporate mission…and it differs a lot from the vision.

There are always different ways to describe a work. You can say that working in the automobile industry is to stamp metal sheet or to build a car or to help others to travel. By widening the scope and giving perspectives, it reinforces the meaning of each job.

Immediately, the nature of the job changes and it can trigger employees' engagement.

A few years ago, I was working in South Africa as managing director of a factory manufacturing drugs for animals. Some of our colleagues were weighing powders; other were mixing liquids and filling bottles. I explained to all of them that their mission was not to mix or weigh or fill or stamp but it was actually about saving an animals life. To illustrate my point, I was converting for all employees, every month, the number of bottles and drums that we sold into numbers of animal lives saved. It was a small initiative but it was a positive change about the way they feel about their job. And it was the same mission for everybody in the organization. Whatever level you have in the company, we were all sharing the same mission; it was about saving the animals life.

A few years later, I was working as a consultant in Thailand for a small company selling perfumes. The company is manufacturing perfumes under its own brand and distributes them through its own shops. During our first discussion with the company founder, we discussed the company mission. I asked him to take some distance from the obvious – we are manufacturing and selling perfumes. We finally agree that the mission would actually be to help women to feel more beautiful. Yes, perfumes do not do the entire job but selling perfumes contribute to this mission.

When we communicated this new mission to the sales staff, we noticed a change in their behaviors over a period of a few days. They started to pay much more attention to the way they dress. They started asking questions to the customers outside the perfumes.

They were asking what events the perfume was for, what type of clothes will they wear or what type of make-up they would use it with. They even brought beauty magazines to the shops to illustrate for each perfume the style of clothes to be associated with.

All these initiatives came naturally from the sales team without any directions from the management. They were showing signs of engagement as they wanted to contribute to the mission they joined. It enriched the relationship between the sales team and their customers. Just by redefining the mission…

INDUSTRIES	MISSION
a Baseball Club	We are providing memories to our fans
a Pharmaceutical company	We are saving life or offering comfort
Walt Disney Amusement Park	We are in the happiness business

During a visit to the NASA space center in 1962, President John F. Kennedy noticed a janitor carrying a broom. He interrupted his tour, walked over to the man and said, "Hi, what is your job about?"

"Well, Mr. President," the janitor responded, "I'm helping put a man on the moon."

To the naked eye, this janitor was just cleaning the building, but in the more mythic, larger story unfolding around him, he was helping put a man on the moon.

Here's the point: No matter how large or small your role, you are contributing to the larger story unfolding within your life, your business, and your organization.

And when your entire team embraces that type of attitude and belief system, incredible things happen.

The mission alone is not sufficient to get a team to engage but it is the starting point. The vision is supposed to be coming from the corporate mission. The mission defines the field of activities. The vision will define the ambition within the mission.

There is often a misunderstanding between mission and vision. The mission statement is a description of what the company is currently doing. A vision statement is a description of what success will mean for the employees in the future. Companies often mix them up and miss their point. If you had to choose only one statement, the vision is more important than the mission.

Mission characterizes an industry while the vision is specific to a team within that industry.

I had a discussion one day with a large US multinational. They wanted to rework their vision. Their vision was "We are feeding the world". I had to explain to them that this is actually a mission. It defines how today they are contributing to their society but it does not illustrate what success would mean tomorrow. What image, comment or number would illustrate that they have been successful in feeding the world? The answer to that question should be their vision.

COMPANY	MISSION [today]	VISION [tomorrow]
Disney Animation Park	We are in the happiness business	We dream that one day our customers will leave the park with smile as big as when they entered
Baseball Club	We are providing memories to our fans	We dream that one day our fans would leave the game and think about who they'll bring to the next game.

4.3 The traps to avoid

4.3.1 - Vision must be designed for employees and not customers or shareholders.

Often, companies want to take this opportunity to deliver a message to their customers about their products and services superiority. Through the exercise, they tend to forget to engage their employees. The main purpose of the vision is to propose an attractive future for employees, not customers. Leaders should not mix up both exercises but create separate statements; one for employees, one for customers and one for shareholders if required.

-- If you find a vision on a public website, it rather is a marketing slogan than an engaging vision --

In one of the previous company I worked for, I was discussing with our CEO about our company vision. He mentioned to me that the vision was very clear "We want to grow 2% faster than the market". I objected that such vision was not very exciting for employees. It is not necessarily mean anything for them, especially if there are not in sales and they would not know how to measure it. He answered to me that he had to provide something attractive for the shareholders. Such a statement would not contribute to engaging employees. It may satisfy shareholders but employees would need something else.

4.3.2 - Vision does not have to be too far in the future

We often believe that vision needs to be defined for the next 10 to 20 years. Actually, the term should be long enough to appear feasible but not too long to keep contributors engaged. The term will depend on the nature of the vision. Do not forget that vision is the synonym of the project. Every project is a vision. It can be a 6-month project, a 12-month or a 3-year one.

Vision aims at breaking up monotony and routine. To maintain a high level of engagement and alignment, employees should always feel in project mode with a clear goal in mind. Once they finish a project, they should move to another project. Each project can last a few months to a few years. The vision is the definition of each project delivery.

Remember to keep your team engaged in exciting projects. If the project that is involved in is not exciting, create new projects that they could be excited about.

4.3.3 - Vision should be emotionally engaging and visible to employees

To engage employees, we need to propose a vision that speaks to them. It is a talent of the leader to understand his team's motives and touch them through the definition of his vision. In most of the case, efficient vision makes employees proud. Pride is the most efficient feeling to fuel efforts towards well-defined goals. We often see vision built on ambitions of market share, sales milestones or market position. It may work for Pepsi employees who dream about taking over Coca-Cola. It may seduce as well as business owners and board directors but it may not mean that much for all employees. It would be better to identify measurement that would be visible for all employees like a change in customers' behaviors.

"I dream that one day all or a part of our customers do something illustrating that we have changed our market…"

When I was working in the pharmaceutical industry, I was the head of Asia. We had 8 subsidiaries in 7 different Asia countries. Our contribution to the group sales was only 5%, lower than what Asia should represent. I decided to define our vision as "Asia will change our company's future". I knew that all employees would like the idea that our subsidiaries would gain importance in our group. There is in most the Asian countries a real motive and pride to shine in front of US and European countries. I gave several examples of what it would be in term of sales contribution (10% of sales), in term of supply (get our factories to export to the US and Europe), in term of marketing (get our marketing concepts and visuals to be reused by US and European subsidiaries) and even in term of management (get an Asian at our European company board). It really became a common agenda for all our teams and it was motivating everything we were initiating.

4.3.4 - Vision is a story, not only a slogan

Do not focus on a slogan. It is indeed a nice way to be impactful and memorable but it is too often limiting, both in the storytelling of the vision and its memorization. Vision is first a story. It has to be detailed. It can be as long as you want. You can even have several visions, several stories. What is important is to be engaging, inspiring and to create a purpose for triggering the changes that we expect in our present. And if you can find a few words slogan to illustrate it, it is even better.

4.4 The cascade of vision

Once defined, the vision needs to be explained clearly and relentlessly repeated to all stakeholders in the organization. Managers need to understand the company vision and explain it regularly to their staff. Every opportunity is good to remind it during the meeting, speeches, employees' award ceremony and especially the employee performance review (cf chapter 6.7).

Several visions can actually cohabit in the same company, as there are several projects. There is definitively a company project to which managers can add their own department's project. An employee can be engaged into several visions at the same time. The financial manager of a company can / should develop a vision of what should be a successful financial department. All his team would participate to two (or more) projects in parallel. In a company, you can have a vision for the marketing department, manufacturing, from team A or B or for a subsidiary. The team vision may have a narrower scope but it will be more meaningful and visible to his team members than the group one.

Many organizations I worked for were exclusively focusing on a unique vision, the one from the CEO. It is indeed CEO's responsibility to propose the directions through a clear vision. But it has never been said that he should be the only one to propose a vision.

I, actually, encourage every manager to propose their own vision for their department. It can be a 3-year, 1-year or a 6-month vision depending on each situation. They must transform their job routine into an exciting project that they believe is realistic and ambitious and whose success will touch participants' pride and they must articulate it into the company vision

An organization leadership architecture is not only made of one vision but it actually contains all the visions/projects that have been defined by various leaders in the organization and that together will drive participants' engagement and alignment. Each of them is a reason for employees to get engaged.

4.5 The butterfly effect

The essence of your vision is to engage your team and to do so, it must be effectively communicated so that it becomes part of your team references. When well understood, a good vision will make employees visualize the landing point of their effort. It gives a direction and most importantly a meaning to their daily job. It is the why behind their effort.

Every opportunity must be seized to repeat and explain the vision; it can be a speech, an email, a board at the office entrance, a meeting, etc…

Great leaders are not only excellent at building vision stories, but they are outstanding in the way they communicate them. Abilities to share the passion and appeal to supporters are key qualities of leaders.

But if we want this vision to mean something for employees, leaders must go one step further and explain how every employee's job connects to the big picture. Participants must understand clearly how their success will impact the company's long-term vision.

Employees in a large corporation often believe that their impact on overall results is negligible. This is partly the reason why they do not care much as anyway their effort would be meaningless and unnoticed. It is leaders' job to convince them otherwise. Imagine if all employees in a large organization would make their job 5% faster with 5% fewer mistakes, can you imagine how faster would process be executed and how the team would overperform. But once again, why should they do it?

We need to explain to each employee how to see his or her contribution to the company success. We will explain to a receptionist that reducing the unanswered calls by 1 per day would increase company credibility that could generate sales through better referencing which ultimately enable the company to reach our vision.

Employees may not see how complex and interconnected all the company processes are. They may not realize that not answering a call or sending a courier to the wrong person or not providing sufficient assistance to a customer can change everything. It is true that when isolated, such an event may appear insignificant. But it would resonate differently if replaced in the context of the vision.

If the leader has done an effective job in engaging employees in the project's vision and if the leader explained connections between all processes, employees will naturally want to positively contribute to a long-term goal that they find exciting. Only then, we will demonstrate the butterfly effect; meaning that a small effort from everybody can bring about outstanding results.

Employees may have difficulties to see the entire picture. They have only a part of the information. The leader has access to the complete picture and it becomes his responsibility to connect all stakeholders in a meaningful and constructive way. Such a task is indeed the most time consuming one for a leader. Designing the component of his leadership may take a few months but keeping all employees engaged and aligned is a daily job. He must target every employee, for every process, every day. It is a critical task for which the leader must dedicate sufficient time together with his team if he does not want them to disengage over time.

Mission and Vision are definitively the foundation of our leadership architecture on which we will build the other 3 elements that we will detail in the following pages. If you stop at this stage, you will only get nice stories without real influence on your team behaviors. It is too often what happens in large organizations. The mission and vision are posted on the wall of the main office without direct connections to everybody daily job.

4.6. The importance of the strategy

"Strategy is about making choices; it's about deliberately choosing to be different. More important than what to do, it is about being clear about what not to do" - Michael Porter

This book is not about strategy. I am not intending to get into details of the elaboration of strategic plan but I would like to demonstrate how the communication of the strategic plan can reinforce the leadership architecture when it is done properly or harm it when it is misused.

When I worked with leaders, I asked them to send me their set of strategic documents. It includes a 5-year plan, annual budget, strategic review, SWOT analysis, etc...My contribution is to identify in these materials the elements that will reinforce the leadership architecture of the organization. I am actually looking for four specific dimensions that strategic summary can reinforce; Vision congruence, Team alignment, Team confidence, Team identity

4.6.1 Vision congruence

It sounds obvious at this stage of the book to mention that all the strategic contents need to support the achievement of the company or the department or the team vision. We need to ensure a minimum congruence in the process. If we want to appear authentic when we are swearing about our vision, we need to show that our decisions and choices support it. It is an exercise of truth that it is not always easy especially in a context that may change rapidly.

When it happens that some decisions may appear inconsistent in relation to the long-term of short-term vision, we need to make a special effort in explaining the reasons behind our choices. Otherwise, our sincerity of the long-term true motive may be questioned by our colleagues.

4.6.2 Team Re-alignment

In most of the companies I consulted for, the budgets and targets are decided from the top management for the rest of the organization. Employees do not have much ownership of these targets. In case they miss the targets, they may feel that anyway the targets were set too high. And there is no way to check whether this is correct or not.

We saw earlier that leaders have the responsibility to build alignment among their team. Such alignment starts with the preparation of the strategies and the definition of the targets. It has to be a bilateral discussion to ensure that it remains as ambitious as possible in the view of the management and as realist as possible in the eyes of the persons in charge of the execution.

We will see this mechanism more in details when we will look at the performance management system. I recommend sending a white paper to the employee to ask them to set their targets by themselves. That requires first an effective communication of the vision to be sure that employees are already engaged. If they are already passionate about the company project, they will know the level of targets to set in order to make the vision become reality. If at the opposite, the level of objectives that they propose is not ambitious enough, that underlines that alignment is not there yet and that the leader must re-engage the employees into his vision.

We do not have many opportunities to align our colleagues. The preparation of strategies is a perfect exercise to obtain everybody support. It is actually a good exercise of validation. Instead of forcing our way in by imposing our view to our colleagues, we should listen to their position. It will enable us to understand what we missed and what we can do better to get them 'excited' by the project vision that we are proposing.

4.6.3   Team Confidence

If we are looking for our employee's support in executing a plan, it is important to obtain first their support. Nobody will support a project that does not have any chances of success. Before deciding to get into an adventure, we all need to understand "what is the plan".

The clearer will be the plan and the more confident will be our supporters. By increasing the perceived chances of success, we will build up our supporters' faith and get them to engage in our project with a higher level of energy and commitment. At the opposite, if leaders do not do sufficient job at convincing them about the relevance of the plan, supporters will be reluctant to join their fate to our project. They may feel that the risk is too high for them to be associated with a failing project.

4.6.4 Team Identity

People like the feeling that they are changing the present for a better future. They want to be told that they are participating in something unique. The communication of the strategy is the opportunity to underline to them how the path they chose is different from the traditional approach. By underlining the differences, we will reinforce supporters' pride and thus reinforce their attachment to the project.

The more different, unique, original will be the vision and the strategy and the higher sense of identity will be built among the team. At the opposite, a classical vision and a common strategy will not enable the leaders to attract supporters and obtain their full support. Why should we care if we just copy everyone else?

For the leader, it is an exercise of communication to build a positive perception about the choices he (and his team) made. He needs to build up employees' pride and sense of belongingness by reinforcing the uniqueness, differences, originality, and sense of contributing to something important. The leader must necessarily adapt his message to each audience he is facing.

The situation can change and strategies can be adjusted. But at each moment of time, the employees must know that there is a captain in charge. Nobody likes indecisiveness and employees need to be constantly reassured that we have a strong plan. Confidence and identity must be leaders' priority when they are communicating their strategy.

Practically, I am recommending leaders to identify from their strategic reviews, budgets or project proposals, any numbers or elements that can either reinforce the statement about the vision and/or convince employees about the feasibility of the vision and/or stress out the originality of your approach. All these elements should be gathered into a specific document that I call the "Strategic story" to be designed for and shared to employees.

In the organization, the most challenging obstacle is not the design of mission, vision or strategic story but it is their execution. In a survey organized by Fortune magazine, 82% of Fortune 500 CEO's feel their organization did an effective job of strategic planning. Only 14% of the same CEO's indicated that their organization did an effective job of implementing the strategy. If leadership is about changes, culture is certainly its biggest resistance and leaders need to manage it correctly if they want to be effective in realizing their vision through the implementation of their strategy.

5. How leaders shape team culture?

5.1 What is the corporate culture?

A culture is the specific collection of values and norms that are shared by groups in an organization and that control the way they interact with each other and with stakeholders outside the organization. The orientation of the culture is highly correlated to the ability of the teams to implement the strategy defined. A large part of the leader activity should be focused on the nurture of the organization culture. By encouraging the proper behaviors, the leader will create a favorable context for execution.

We all spontaneously behave according to our beliefs grouped into 2 concepts; values and norms.

Values; what we consider critically important for us

Norms; what we believe worked in the past for us

Our prioritization of values are the results of years of education. We choose first what we believe in without being able to explain why. If you can explain why it is not a value. 'Hard work' is for example not a value as we often have a motive for working hard. You normally do not have motives for being honest, it is just that you do not feel uncomfortable when you are facing dishonesty.

The norms are actually the habits that we developed over the years because they worked for us or for our eldest in the past; a certain way to speak, to walk, to say hello, etc…We tend to stick to them to avoid leaving our comfort zone.

Example of values; respect, integrity, improvement, teamwork, safety, authenticity, honesty, communication, responsibility, innovation, entrepreneurship, empowerment, quality, sustainability, results orientated, ambition, curiosity, objectivity, professionalism, diversity, productivity, adaptability, reliability, customer drive, fairness, transparency, accountability.

If you want to do a small exercise with your colleagues about culture, ask them to pick 5 values among the list above and to rank them by order of importance. Then you compare the results to yours to understand better the difference of culture and therefore behaviors in a group.

More than the selection of the values themselves, the order is important. Companies often offer a list of 5-7 values to define their culture. To be more precise, we should actually rank them in order of importance. When taking a decision, our brain is indeed looking for a solution that will match the value 1 and then look at the value 2, etc... If two persons select the same values but in a different order, they may end up taking different decisions and adopting different behaviors in front of a similar situation.

Both our values rank and norms dictate the way we behave and interact at our work.

But in our organization, we are not alone. We are part of a team with colleagues coming from different horizons with different education and history. Our behavioral patterns (the way we rank values and beliefs) are naturally different at first.

When we do not react to a situation the way our colleague would do, that can trigger some frustrations and ultimately some tensions, which could damage the cohesion and effectiveness of the team. To minimize such tensions, it is important to share the same behavioral patterns. If possible, we would prefer to encourage behaviors that will support the most efficiently the business to realize the team vision. The organizational leader is in charge of understanding each individual culture and readjusts his or her behaviors in line with the culture that he wants to promote.

To do so, he needs to clearly define what are the expected values, norms and behaviors that he wants to become the references.

"I came to see, in my time at IBM, that culture isn't just one aspect of the game, it is the game. In the end, an organization is nothing more than the collective capacity of its people to create value." – Louis Gerstner, IBM

I would like to share as well three other definitions that may be less formal but more illustrative

"Culture is the way things are done in an organization". This encompasses all the practices and behaviors that an organization develops over time. It takes time for an outsider to capture it. There is this unique identity of every organization that is hard to imitate.

"Culture reflects the lessons learned that were important enough to pass to the next generation". It includes all the wisdom that resisted to the time to characterize the ways things work in an organization.

"Culture is what we do when nobody is looking". This sentence underlines that our behaviors are driven by inner motives back from our education and background. This definition reinforces as well that culture cannot be imposed by authority. It would require to 'sell' the new behaviors by explaining to the team that it is a requirement for the team to achieve the vision defined together.

5.2 Reference behaviors

Companies often define a list of values and they consider that it is sufficient to realign all stakeholders on the desired culture. It is definitively not sufficient. Leaders need to do much more than that.

It is important to rank values as we mentioned earlier and we must translate the values into behaviors in a way that everybody can understand. We must select visible behaviors that can be noticeable by co-workers. We should avoid empty paraphrases to underline evidence.

Examples of behaviors not sufficiently explicit

VALUES	BEHAVIORS
Integrity	Act and communicate with integrity
Respect	Treat everyone with respect and courtesy
Team Work	Together with your team you could achieve more
Honesty	Be honest in all your dealings
Quality	Engage the right people with the right experience

It is not an exercise of vocabulary. We are not asking necessarily to copy the definition from the dictionary. It is an opportunity to describe the associated behaviors that you would like to become a reference in our organization.

VALUES	BEHAVIORS
Team Work	In the team interest, we will not hesitate to challenge any decision of the team. Once the decision is made we will support it, even if it is differerent from our point of view
Innovation	We will not accept past practices as rules but must always propose better solutions
Respect	We will never aggress physically, verbally, emotionally colleague, whatever are our motivations.
Solidarity	Helping out our team mate must be accepted as a mission, even if it's not formally mentioned in our job scope
Commitment	We will not stop unless our objective is reached
Performance	We will measure our performance on the capacity to deliver not to perform a task
Responsibility	We are always responsible for our actions. It is about what we can do and not what others did

In the table above, you will notice that I took some liberty in the transcription of the value into behaviors. The objective is to select behaviors that are tangible. We should include a verb of action. It is about doing something and not about thinking or being somebody.

5.3 The contribution of legends

To be fully understood, the behaviors need to be translated into practical examples. These examples have to be adapted to each position in the organization to be sure that employees visualize correctly the behaviors. The exercise consists in building a list of small stories, real or imaginary that we call legends. It can take several years to build all these stories.

The leader should then use these legends regularly when he wants to illustrate a behavior. There should be at least one legend associated with each behavior for each department. All the legends may not come from the company's head but each department's head should take the liberty to add their own legends to contribute with practical examples close to the reality of his department.

BEHAVIORS	LEGENDS
We always get prepared	We prepare in advance answers to questions that can be asked to us
	We always ask the agenda before joining a meeting
	We always collect information about customers prospects before meeting them
When we see something is 'wrong, we do something for it …until we see it is correct.	When we see a stain on the wall, we should inform the relevant person and ensure that it is corrected
We handle details as if it is the center of attention because it makes the difference	When we visit a customer, we ensure that you bring ALL the accessories to deliver a consistent image about our company
We will consistently look for better solutions wihout accepting past practices as rules	We will never say something because we are used to do it. We must do it because we are convinced it is the best way to do it

5.4 How do leaders build / reinforce / change corporate culture?

A new culture will always face resistance from the previous culture. Even when a team is composed for the first time, each member is coming with his own culture and will resist the new culture…because it is not necessarily what is important for him (his values) and because it is not necessarily what used to work for him (his beliefs). Therefore, to impact the organizational culture, the leaders will have to work hard at communicating the new culture.

The communication will cover 3 dimensions; formal, behavioral and decisional.

5.4.1 Formal

The culture should indeed be formally shared with all employees through all possible supports available for internal communication. It should be reserved only for employees and not targeting any commercial purpose. It should as well target all the employees of the organization and not only designed for the 'happy few'.

Leaders need to use the behaviors and legends as references. These stories must be regularly reminded to employees to comment or reflect on employees daily behaviors. It is up to the leaders to make the culture alive in the organization.

5.4.2 Behavioral

Leaders should match their own behaviors on the ones defined in the culture. This is the most efficient channel of communication. Leaders should lead by example. We cannot convince about the importance of specific behavior if we do not apply to ourselves.

Leaders are constantly observed by their team and every action and declaration will be scrutinized in order to check whether they are consistent with their words. As soon as an inconsistency is found, credibility and sincerity of leaders will be questioned. Sometimes, only one inconsistency is sufficient to destroy all the model credibility.

---We watch leaders move their feet not move their lips---

Communication, respect, integrity, and excellence were the values of ENRON at the time the scandal was discovered. Putting nice words on a board is definitively not sufficient to impact positively the business.

Leaders must be very disciplined to stick to the reference behaviors they have set themselves. They must be seen in their daily behaviors. Because of their exposure, leaders are naturally the ambassadors of the organization culture. They must be the first and most disciplined adopter.

"You must be the change you wish to see in the world" - Gandhi

5.4.3 Decisional

Finally, the last driver for the leader to impact the organizational culture is the decisions that he will take especially in the 4 areas listed below

Leader agenda

Time is supposed to be the most precious leaders' resources and the way leaders allocate it says a lot on their priorities. If a leader wants to communicate a priority to his team, he must be sure that he allocates the proper proportion of his time by attending the related meeting and/or asking regular questions about that topic.

Frequency is more important than intensity. Leaders will make a stronger point by asking the same question several times at regular frequency rather than making a big noise one time. I call it the 'Monday morning question'. If you ask the same question every Monday morning to your team over time, they will start realizing how important that topic is for you and they will adjust their behaviors accordingly. But you need to be consistent. If you stop asking the question without credible explanation, they will conclude that it was finally not that important for you

The frequency of a question clearly indicates that the topics stay on the top of leaders' mind and therefore that it is something important that should be focused on.

Positive behaviors should be recognized

It is critical for the process to reinforce positive behaviors by celebrating them when they occur. Such celebration will be an opportunity to share among the team some more examples of how behaviors are exercised in the job. It will contribute to enriching the legends in the organization by adding more illustration of how we do things here.

It will give as well a strong message to the team that such behaviors are encouraged by the leaders and should become the reference behaviors.

The best way to encourage behaviors is to recruit candidates with it. The hiring interview should give a priority to identify the values, beliefs, and behaviors of candidates. It is not only an efficient way to enrich the team but it is as well a strong message to give to the rest of the team

Negative behaviors should be systematically fought

It is even more important to fight against negative behaviors. For the same reason that above, we need to provide a clear illustration to the team about what is acceptable and what is not acceptable.

And this is actually, the real test for the culture. In some situation, punishing or firing an employee because of repeated negative behaviors can be a difficult decision, especially if that employee is performing well. But this is a moment where the leader will show how much behaviors are important to him. Such decision may be costly for him and the organization but it will give a strong message to the rest of the team.

Progress needs to be measured

As Lou Gerstner mentioned it in his book "Who says Elephants can't dance?" about his experience in changing IBM culture, to really get your team attention on the desired change, we need to make it visible to them and others through measurement.

"People don't do what you expect but what you inspect" – Lou Gerstner – IBM CEO

It is possible to measure the compliance of employees to selected behaviors. We will have a complete chapter on that topic. Measuring compliance is first a strong way to insist on the importance of the behaviors we want to promote. If we are serious about measuring them, employees will understand that we are serious about implementing them. Moreover, the measurement will enable to quantify expectations and celebrate progress.

5.5 What is a good culture?

Every organization claims to have a good and strong culture. But what does that mean? Should we conclude that other organizations have a 'bad' culture?

Every individual and organization has a culture. They believe in values from their education and they follow norms accumulated by experience. The most relevant question is rather to know whether this culture is equally shared by all team members and whether it supports the team strategy.

The culture needs to be absorbed by all group members and not only a few individuals to become a characteristic of the whole organization. If we want the culture to impact the behaviors of the organization, it must be shared by all individuals.

During my consultations, I often question both management and employees about their culture "What behaviors would you like to encourage and what behaviors do you want to banish from your organization". Through this exercise, I often measure the gap between different parts of the organization. Culture is rarely well shared and understood and there are always additional efforts required to make to get the culture better deployed.

When well-designed, the culture will support the strategy but it will contribute as well to reinforce team identity and employee loyalty. Once employees follow the same patterns of behaviors in front of a given situation, these patterns are becoming part of the team identity and it is reinforcing binding between employees. They start to feel comfortable with each other and collaboration is getting more efficient.

Roy E. Disney (Co-founder of Walt Disney company) once said, "Once the culture is clear, decisions are easy". By defining ways of doing business, by setting guiding principles, the leaders are bringing predictability to the decision making process. The decision grid is shared by the team and the conclusions are understood and supported.

More than that, once the culture well established and employees comfortable with a certain way of doing things, they will start correcting each other behaviors when they believe their colleagues do not follow 'the way'. We are establishing a 'social control' that can then replace the hierarchical control. Culture brings predictability on the behaviors and once management trusts the power of the culture, they can start releasing hierarchical control and giving more freedom for employees to take initiatives. Such empowerment will increase employee satisfaction, as they can get ownership of their decisions. By trusting the power of well designed and aligned culture, we are releasing energies and empowering employees

6.

The importance of execution

6.1 Our leadership architecture

The end game of every leader is to have an impact on his organization. It is about execution and results. It is indeed a very different thing to set a relevant mission, compelling vision, a wise strategy, a clear culture model and to translate them into proper and timely actions. By communicating his leadership platform, the leader sets the scene but he must then ensure that the plan is executed.

I summarized the leadership model in a diagram where I represented both the leadership square and the management square. The manager has the mission to execute the directions given by the leader. The leader sets the goals and the manager ensures to achieve them by coaching talents, building organization & processes and driving behaviors. The leadership square includes the 4 pillars that we described earlier; mission, vision, strategy, and culture. All of them end up in performance.

The performance management is indeed a key process both for leadership and management square. It is crystallizing the elements from the strategy on one side and the culture on the other side. It is not the only way to communicate vision, strategy, and culture but it is the most formal and generally the most impactful way to drive change of behaviors and build motives for employees.

6.2 The theory of motivation

Many sociologists have been working on the motivation theory, from Ernest Mayo, Abraham Maslow, and his famous pyramid or Frederick Herzberg with his theory of motivation.

All of them arrived at similar conclusions but they illustrated it in a different way.

In his work, Herzberg classified 3,597 situations at work into 2 groups; the ones that brought satisfaction to employees and the ones who brought dissatisfaction. For each of them, he interviewed the employees to understand the reasons behind their satisfaction or dissatisfaction.

He noticed that in the "satisfied" group, 40% of the motives were a sense of achievement. "Success" is the main motive of satisfaction in that study. The second motive of satisfaction is "recognition" in 30% of the cases. Comes then the nature of the job, job responsibility, job advancement, and personal growth.

Salary is mentioned in less than 10% of the cases. Salary is indeed a key element for an employee to join a company. But it is then a given and will not drive employee satisfaction and motivation in daily life. Bonus or reward will impact employee motivation partly because it is a promise of increased quality of life but as well because the bonus is most of the time associated with success and recognition.

The other factors below have little chance to create high motivation when they are fulfilled. They were mentioned by the participants in a few cases only. At the opposite, when these factors were not fulfilled, they were the reasons for the high level of dissatisfaction.

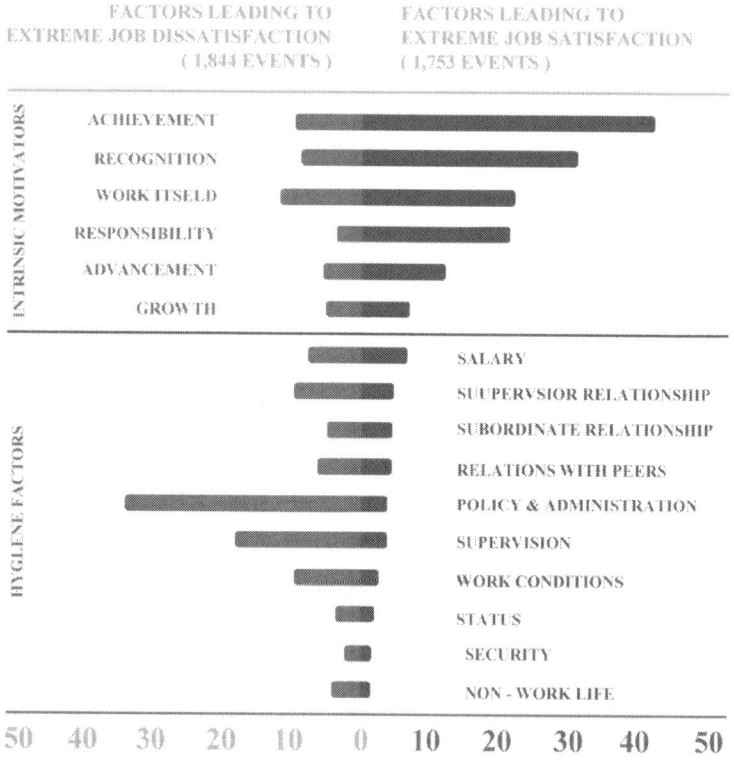

Strict Company Policy, tight supervision or insufficient work conditions have been listed by participants as being major reasons for frustration in the events covered by the study.

Herzberg made, therefore, a distinction between the HYGIENE factors and the MOTIVATION factors. We call HYGIENE factors the ones that had a negative influence on employees' satisfaction when not perceived at an acceptable level by the employees. The MOTIVATION factors are the ones that could be a source of satisfaction and engagement when well leveraged in an organization.

If you want to get your employees highly motivated and engaged in a project, you need to ensure that the context is favorable for achievement, success, recognition, responsibility, advancement, and growth. The importance of learning, personal development, increased responsibility, career progression has been discussed many times and I will not spend more time on these. But let us be honest, such drivers of motivation are not possible for everybody in the organization. There are only a few management positions in an organization and budget for personal development is limited. These drivers can be leveraged only on few 'happy' ones. At the opposite, success and recognition are accessible for everybody and it is free. It only requires time and attention from the organization leaders.

Hygiene factors should not be ignored in an organization. They can prevent engagement if employees are in the red zone. Leaders must handle these points wisely in order to reach the minimum acceptable. But there is no point in over-investing in these areas. That will not drive satisfaction. The best you will get is to prevent employees from complaining.

Employees complain because of insufficient working conditions but they do not engage in their job because they have a nice office. They will complain if their job does not offer security but they will not engage further if their organization offer them a secured position.

At the opposite, success can become addictive and if the system places employees into a successful environment, they may even ask for more. It can become a virtuous circle providing that the system brings sufficient objectivity and that leaders reinforce the cycle with sufficient recognition of employees' success.

In Sport, Religion and many other fields, we have multiple examples of women and men who realize outstanding performance by the only motive of success and recognition. These two drivers are actually huge potential energy inside each of us that only wait for us or somebody else to call for it.

I participated in the past years to many performance reviews and I was often surprised by the way managers to handle this exercise. This is a unique opportunity for the managers to celebrate success and recognize contribution in order to press the button of engagement. It is a required step in the motivation cycle. If we want our colleagues to get onboard again into a new cycle, they must feel good about it. Money is not a sufficient leverage, it is important to add up success and recognition. They often missed this chance by being too much focus on the results rather than the driver of the performance. By not pushing the right button, they were setting up their team for failure.

But the success celebration and recognition must stay sincere, consistent and meaningful if the leaders want to stay credible. The leader must make a special effort of objectivity for the evaluation to be meaningful.

6.3 We get only what we measure

To get attention from your team on the results to deliver, it is important to make the expected changes visible. By measuring progress on specific areas, you are first showing that you care about the deliverables that you are expecting but more importantly, you are making your team accountable for the results. They will know that results will be monitored and that the only way to be successful and recognized by others as such will be to deliver.

Measurement enables us to clarify our expectations. We often consider that we have been clear in our explanations and that we are understood. When I visit companies, I generally start my consultation by organizing interviews with both leaders and some employees selected randomly in the organization. I am asking them the same questions about the company missions, vision, strategies, culture, and goals and I often surprised by the level of misunderstanding in the answers I get. These persons have often been working together for years but they are still misaligned. This exercise is very useful to understand misalignment in an organization and it is the job of the leader to work this out by getting much more precise and quantitative on the goals of each employee.

By making the performance objective and visible, you are creating a positive context for employees to achieve. We must simply ensure that the measurement is objective and meaningful.

I spent a lot of time in the animal feed industry. One of the most important processes in this industry is the feed formulation. The formulators are adjusting regularly the formulas taking into account customers' feedback and raw materials price variation in order to maximize feed efficiency and reduce feed cost. It is a critical process for these companies but they rarely measure its performance. The natural attitude of formulators is to avoid taking any risk. If there is a problem in the feed after they adjust it, everybody will blame them. At the opposite, when they take initiatives in order to reduce costs or increase feed efficiency, nobody will recognize it as it is not monitored. The cost will be reduced but we will not know whether it is the results of the reduction of raw materials price or an adjustment of the formula. As a result, formulators are becoming reluctant to risks and may miss some chances of creating more value for their company.

When we implemented the FPI project (Formulation Performance Index), we created a measurement visible to management and to all their colleagues. It gave a strong message to the formulation team about what was expected from them and a strong motive for the formulator to outstretch themselves. Their contribution was emphasized and that encourages the team to raise up their standards.

I have a similar experience in another company around purchasing. It is not an easy task to measure the performance in the purchase as benchmarks are always relative to a context. But we found relevant objectives and we noticed a change of behaviors in the purchasing department. That created some inspirations as they had some goals to beat in order to be recognized in the organization in the same way that salespeople are celebrated.

6.4 The road map

You will find below the template that I developed and I am using in my consulting job. This table is named Road Map; map as it is picturing the way we will measure the performance as objectively as possible and road because it must give a direction in relation with the mission, vision, strategies, and culture as presented earlier.

We do not have one table but actually two. The first document is the roadmap as illustrated below. It is only measuring the strategic targets that we expect the employee to deliver at the end of each period. It is actually a quantification of the points where the employee agrees to land. The second document is measuring the performance related to the behaviors as described in the organization culture. We will come back on it in the next chapter.

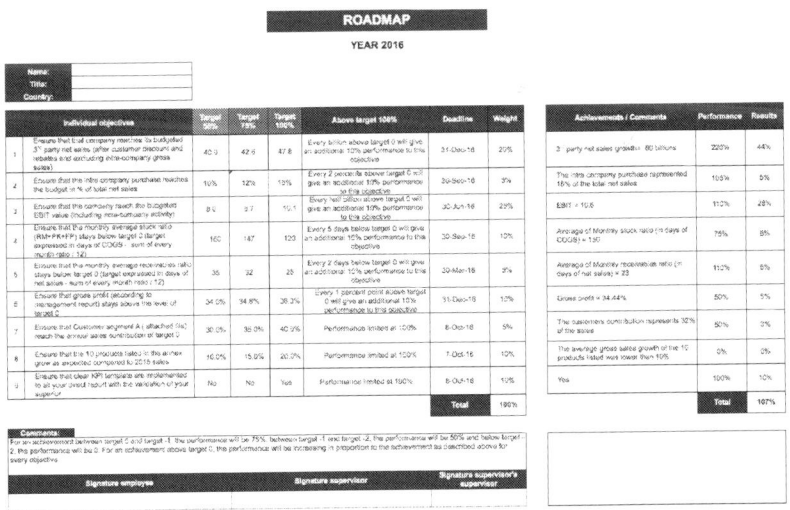

(cf annex 3)

The template must clearly identify the following elements;

- Employee details
- Period covered
- List of objectives
- The weight of each objective
- Targets (at least 5 targets for 50%, 75%, 100%, 120% and 150% achievement)
- Results at the end of the period
- Calculation of the overall performance (sum of weighted performance)
- Comments on the performance of the period

There are 3 critical steps that we are going to review together; selection of objectives, the weight of each objective and definition of targets.

6.4.1 - Objectives

The most difficult and critical exercise in all the leadership process that I am presenting in this book is about the selection of objectives. Most businesses are used to measure sales performance by monitoring sales, margin, expenses or profit. Those are the easy ones.

It is more difficult to implement measurement for marketing, production, human resources, logistic, product development, customer services or accounting. We need to select objectives by either using figures that already exists in the organization database or by creating new metrics.

The selection of objectives must follow two simple rules; be measurable objectively (without any judgment) and reflect the strategies

I encourage the manager to build this roadmap together with the employee at the beginning of each cycle. The starting point should be what I call the job mapping. We are asking an employee to describe his job and we help him to connect each mission with one of the 3 main short-term goals of the company;

- Increase Profit
- Reduce Risks
- Optimize Resources

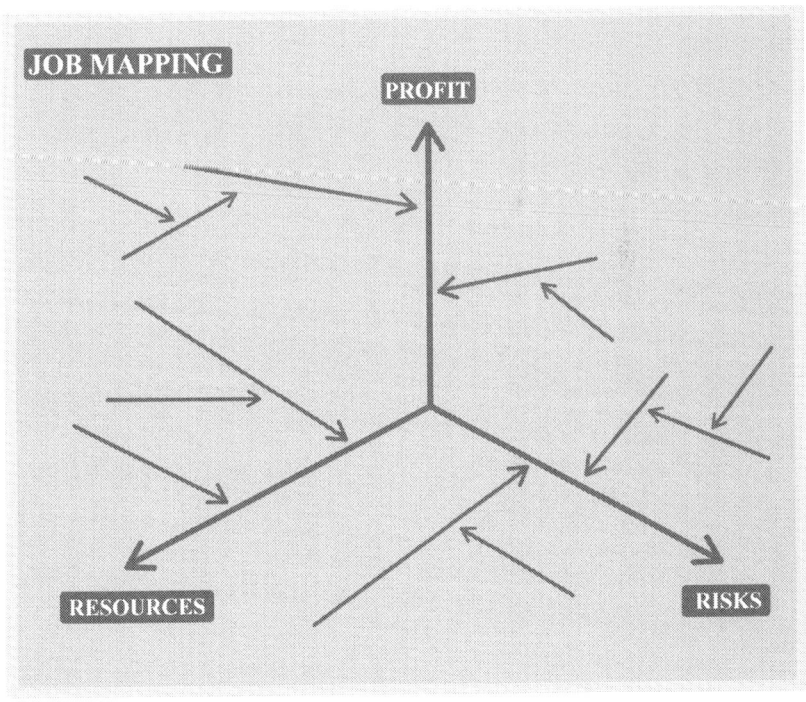

This diagram is actually a tool to organize the discussion between the manager and the employee with a double ambition in mind. First, it is important to give some perspectives for the employee to understand the connection between the objectives that we are going to select and the company mission and vision. This exercise is an opportunity for the leader to re-engage the employee into the company vision and the employee contribution.

I coached many job mapping sessions where the employee did not know at first how he was contributing to the company overall profit, resources and risks management. I remember a session where the employee was explaining to me that she was producing reports that she was sending every month to headquarter but she did not really know how these reports were used. The exercise helped her to understand that the report was helping to take decisions in order to mitigate some specific exposures and that some mistakes on her side could affect the company decision process and therefore the company vision. That gave suddenly a sense of importance and pride to the employee who understood why and how we will measure her performance. For an employee to get engaged in their job, they must fully understand what is their contribution. They must know that their contribution is visible and how they can affect positively or negatively the overall results.

The second purpose of the job mapping is to identify as many points of contribution as possible. Each point of contribution should then be subject to an objective. We should ask ourselves;

"what results do you expect from this mission"

"what deliverables will show that you are successful in realizing this mission"

It is important to be as precise as possible to avoid future misunderstanding. I take the example of training. There are many ways to measure the success of the persons responsible for organizing training. Each one gives a different message.

1. Ensure that the minimum number of training is organizing on the period (to be qualified, a training must gather at least 10 employees for a minimum of 1 hour)
2. Ensure that a minimum number of employees join the training
3. Ensure that a minimum number of persons attend the training (employees can join several different training)
4. Ensure all employees trained to reach an acceptable mark at the post-training test

As an illustration of this chapter, you will find 50 examples of objectives in annex 1. You can find as well hundreds of examples on the web but it is important that you build your own objectives to match the specificity of your context.

Following the job mapping, we normally end up with 10 to 15 points of the contribution that should generate 10 to 15 objectives. We should then select the most relevant one to keep only the 5 to 10 most important.

I want to insist on the importance of clarity. Each word used in the objectives must be clearly defined without leaving any chance of misunderstanding. Do we speak about total on the period or average? Do we speak about net or gross? The experiences show that we often realize at the end of the period when we are measuring the results that both parties were not using the same metrics. It is always better to invest some more time at first in detailing each word definition.

6.4.2 - Weight

The weight illustrates the importance of each objective so that employee understands how it should allocate his time and effort in order to maximize his results. The weight must reflect the company choices. It dictates where employees should focus their effort and attention. The weight must give sufficient information for employees to make arbitration when needed. It often happens that strategies contain antagonist ambitions.

- Increase both sales volume and margin rate
- Increase sales while respecting payment terms
- Increasing production output while reducing quality rejections
- Increasing product performance while reducing costs

The weight associated to each objective enable the employee to know what to put first when taking a decision. They will naturally take the position that will optimize the roadmap results, which should reflect the optimal arbitration as well for the company.

The below example illustrates two possible roadmap scenarios regarding the weight to associate to two contradictory objectives; sales volume and margin rate. The employee can decide to reduce price in order to generate an increase of sales volume, but he will have to accept a reduction of margin rate. Or he can maintain or even increase price in order to improve the margin rate, but it may then be more difficult to generate higher sales.

	Weight Roadmap 1	Weight Roadmap 2
Sales Volume	70%	30%
Margin Rate	30%	70%

We can easily foresee that salesmen will not adopt the same strategy whether he needs to optimize his results from the roadmap 1 or the roadmap 2. The way his leader will define objectives and most importantly the weight of his roadmap will tremendously affect the way he will take a decision in his business. Ideally, the roadmap should be designed as a guideline to enlighten employees on the way we want them to drive the business.

It sounds simple to associate a weight to an objective, but it is actually not that easy. The first reflex would be to split the weight equally between all the objectives, as they are all important. But that is actually a way not to decide. We must force ourselves to make choices. It is one of the most important acts of leadership. We must have the courage to give low weight to secondary objectives in order to stress out the importance of the core objectives.

These weights depend on the context. One objective may have a 30% weight on that quarter but get a lower weight on the next period because the context is different or because the leader wants to emphasize another dimension of the business.

I mentioned earlier that the definition of objectives should be the results of the discussion with the employee. The selection of the weight, on the contrary, must be a unilateral recommendation from the leader. This is the moment where the leader is actually connecting the dots between the micro and the macro picture. He must be sure that the prioritization of the objectives is consistent with the vision and strategies but as well with the roadmap of the other employees.

6.4.3 – Specific or transversal

To measure individual success, the objective must be as specific as possible to underline the effort and contribution of the employee only. The danger of having only specific objectives is that the employee will care only about his own success, sometimes at the cost of another department performance. That way, we may achieve a high level of motivation from employees but create tension between colleagues. Without realizing it, we are then creating a culture of individualism.

At the opposite, if all the objectives are transversal, we are measuring the individual success through the results of a team. To achieve a good performance, the employee will have to collaborate with each other. We are then promoting collaboration, but we will not reach a similar level of motivation and engagement, as employees may tend to let their colleagues make the efforts and benefit from the team results.

I would, therefore, recommend mixing both specific and collective objectives. To obtain the best balance between motivation and collaboration, I suggest getting 70% of the total weight on specific objectives and the remaining 30% on the collective ones.

6.4.4 - Targets

The targets must be the results of a discussion between the manager and the employee. It is very important that the employee feels confident about the realism of the targets. The results should be challenging enough for the performance to be admirable, but they should be realistic for the employee to have faith in their success.

I would recommend that once we agree on the selection and wording of the objectives, we ask the employee to propose the targets by himself first and we discuss them together later. If we, as leaders, have done a good job in engaging employees into the company vision and strategies, the employees will want to contribute to the company success by proposing challenging targets. You may be surprised when employees, fully excited about the project they are part of, propose very challenging targets, higher than the ones you would have set yourselves. We then need to ask them to lower the level of challenges in order to avoid endangering their success.

If according to your own judgment, targets are set too low by the employees, that means he is not as engaged and committed as you are. It is a strong feedback to you as his leader that you need to make a better job in explaining to him what you are trying to achieve as a team and to convince him that he, together with his colleagues, has all the resources and talents to aim higher. You may be disappointed that your team spontaneously do not aim as high as you would. But it is actually an opportunity for you to reinforce your leadership and insist on the 'why'. Without giving him the chances to open up his mind on the set up of his targets, you will have missed the chances to re-engage him. You would have imposed your goals, but you would have been surprised by the lack of accountability when employees fail to meet them. Why should they feel accountable for goals that you set?

The roadmap is often misused. Leaders use this table to calculate the amount of the bonus to distribute. They set high targets either because they are extracted from the budget that has already been made without input from employees or because leaders set a level of targets that they consider employees need to reach to deserve the payment of their bonus. They actually forgot why we are implementing roadmaps. The purpose of the whole exercise is to create a situation of success for employees, to reinforce a positive cycle of motivation and an addiction that will lead employees to engage and commit.

That should be the main intention of all leaders. Whatever the budget you defined, we want all employees to demonstrate a high level of attention, dedication, and commitment to obtain the best results as possible.

I often saw leaders setting high targets considering that it will stretch employees to deliver extra value to the company. It is often the wrong approach as we are minimizing the chances of success for employees. We are creating a culture of failure that will demotivate and disengage the team.

Roadmap must be designed to ensure success. It is a tool for leaders to quantify and celebrate individual achievement. The leader must learn how to set targets in such a way that stretches his team effort while ensuring their success. He must know what level of stretch is still achievable by his team. If a majority of employee fails to achieve their roadmap targets, it means that the leaders set targets too high. I saw some companies where managers had an objective in their roadmap: "Ensure that a majority of your team members achieve more than 100% in their roadmap". It may appear as an encouragement for complacency or a contest of popularity. It is actually smarter than that. The message it gives is that we get the best of our people when they are stretching themselves to achieve their goals. The highest amount of energy comes when we are close to the finish line…the extra effort to cross the line first. To get this energy from your team, they must 'smell' the finish line. They must smell it before the start of the race and during all the races…and if possible, they must enjoy the celebration of victory so that they are eager to the next race. Our job as a leader is to ensure that the 'victory smell' is always there to reinforce engagement. Excellence and productivity is the result of engagement and not the other way around.

Focusing at first on productivity, setting targets as high as possible in order to get our team to aim high is actually counterproductive.

6.5 The Behavioral performance

We stressed earlier the importance of a well-designed culture to support the execution of the strategy. As for the strategy deliverables, it is important to measure the behavioral patterns to encourage compliance.

The measurement takes a different approach than for the roadmap. Behavioral measurement is by nature subjective and must be treated separately. We are using 360° behavioral assessments to confirm whether the employee is perceived by his close colleagues as behaving according to the company cultural standards.

The use of such assessment was still limited in an organization in the past as it was heavy to manage through paper or excel. There is now online software that makes it very simple to deploy (www.kpisoft.com).

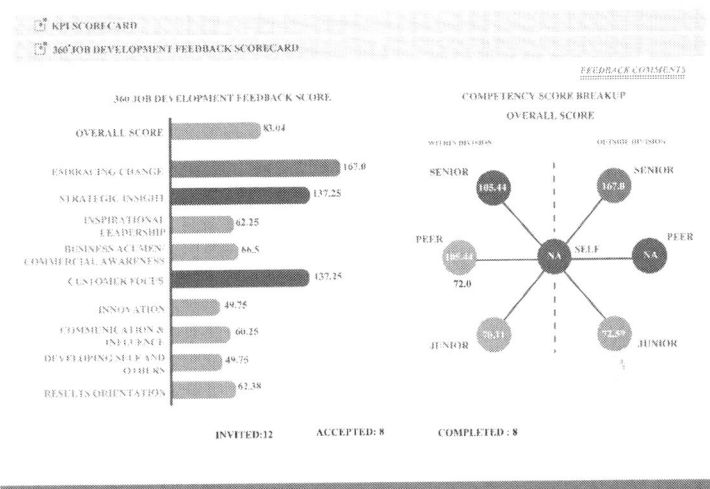

For every employee, we list the colleagues, peers, and superiors that will participate in the survey. We need a minimum of 8 persons to maintain confidentiality. The software will send by email the list of questions to every participant selected and the answers will be computed into an average per topics and overall. It takes 30mn to grade a colleague online and results are produced instantaneously once the last respondent complete the questionnaire.

It is important that the reference questionnaire that we use for the 360° behavioral assessment closely reflects the organization culture and do not copy other companies' model. Indeed, the assessment must be meaningful and connected to the leadership model. There will be no sense to assess employees on Mac Donald's or IBM cultural standards.

We will get a number between 1 and 5. This result from the first assessment does not mean much as the context is too subjective and we must be very careful on the way we are using this number. We should not use it against the respondents if we do not want to kill the process. They are only a starting point from which participants need to improve. We will then start monitoring the evolution as often as possible to measure progress

At the beginning of each period, as for the roadmap, we define a target and coach in details what behaviors to improve and how. The more often we are assessing behavioral performance, the stronger the message we send on the importance of corporate culture and the more change we are driving.

The overall performance of each employee would then be calculated by adding the performance from the roadmap to the performance from the 360 behavioral assessment multiplied by the weight that you want to associate to each of them.

	WEIGHT	PERFORMANCE	WEIGHTED AVERAGE
Roadmap	70%	108%	76%
360° behavioral assessment	30%	98%	29%
		OVERALL PERFORMANCE	105%

We need to be very careful when choosing the proper repartition between the roadmap performance and the behavioral assessment. Here again, this is a strong message we are giving to the organization about our leadership. You will not drive the same behaviors from your team if you explain to them that the roadmap performance will count for 90% of the overall results or if you decide to go for 50%. Both are fine as long as you are aware of what you are communicating and that you stay consistent with the rest of your leadership architecture.

6.6 How to obtain employees buy-in into the performance system?

Like any new system, the implementation of a new performance management system will create resistance from the employees. The main critics that we face are that the system is unrealistic, invasive and too subjective to measure a real performance. Actually, often employees are afraid not to perform.

Without sufficient user acceptance and participation, the system could definitively build up frustration both on the employees and managers side.

The common mistake of leaders is to implement the roadmap without spending sufficient time to introduce it. Leaders must indeed (re-)engage employees into the vision and explain the importance of a proper execution of strategy for the team to succeed. He must insist on the need for accountability and monitoring and introduce the roadmap as a way to celebrate contributors to the company vision for a proper recognition.

Employees must understand that for the team to realize their vision, it is critical to achieving the intermediate milestones defined in the strategy. Achieving targets is called performance and it must be integrated as part of the team culture. Setting objectives, taking accountabilities and accepting the challenges that lie behind each target must be part of accepted rules of the organization.

As any cultural changes, it may take time for employees to accept the new standards and the leader play a big role in getting the message through. He must show to his team that he is determined to monitor performance. He can be flexible on the time required but he must be firm on the landing point.

The lines below will underline the cursors the leader can play with to ensure a progressing deployment of the roadmap and ease users' acceptance.

The first two cycles of roadmap must focus on user acceptance rather than maximization of output. We must, therefore, put employees in a situation of success to give a positive taste of the system and encourage acceptance. After several successes, they will ask for more. At the opposite, the repeated setback would lead them to reject the system.

To increase the chances of success, we will work on the following drivers

Period covered

We may need to start with monthly or quarterly targets and review. In a few months and a few cycles, you will have a faster learning curve in order to select relevant objectives and define better the targets. Thus, the employees will have more chances of succeeding and initial setback will be diluted among the following cycles. If we start from the first cycle for a period of one year, there will not be any chance to recover from a misconception and the learning curve will take 2 to 3 years. Employees will get disengaged long before the end of the process.

Nature of objectives

All the purpose in this exercise is to bring objectivity to performance measurement. We must pay a special attention to design objectives that do not require any judgment. The results must be a number or a date. It may require some external help to design the objectives at first but the system will then work for years.

Depending on the maturity and accountability of each employee, it may be easier to start defining objectives based on the execution of a task (complete a task before the deadline) and with more experiences, move towards deliverables (get results).

Number of objectives and weight of objectives

At maturity, I recommend limiting the number of objectives to 5-7 in order to get a clear focus. But at the beginning, I encourage to set around 10 objectives to dilute possible negative surprises. After a few successful cycles, once the correct objectives and targets will be confirmed, we will then reduce the list to 5-7 objectives.

In case, an objective turns out to be irrelevant on the course of a cycle, we should then report the related weight to another objective.

Targets

Leaders must accept the idea that for the first cycles, the targets should be quite easy to achieve. I remind that we are looking during these first cycles to get users' acceptance. Once the system will be recognized as an operational tool in the organization, the leaders will then be able to increase the level of challenges of the targets.

Ideally, leaders should involve their team in the setting of targets. They should even ask them to propose their targets. They will always be a discussion around targets. It is a constructive discussion that actually reinforces understanding and expectations from both sides. But to minimize gaps and increase alignment, the power of the vision plays a major role. If the vision is attractive enough and if employees understand their role and contribution to the vision, they will naturally want to participate through their achievement.

Achievement / Performance correlation algorithm

In my model, the 50% target is the level of achievement below which we get a 0 performance. This 50% target point must actually be correlated to the difficulties to predict targets.

During the first cycles, when the organization does not have many experiences in setting targets, when the precision is limited, the gap between the target associated to the 50% and the target associated to the 150% mark should be wide to ensure that the lack of precision does not disadvantage too much employees' performance. When precision gets better, the gap between the 50%

and the 150% mark should be narrowed to reflect the gain of experience in setting targets.

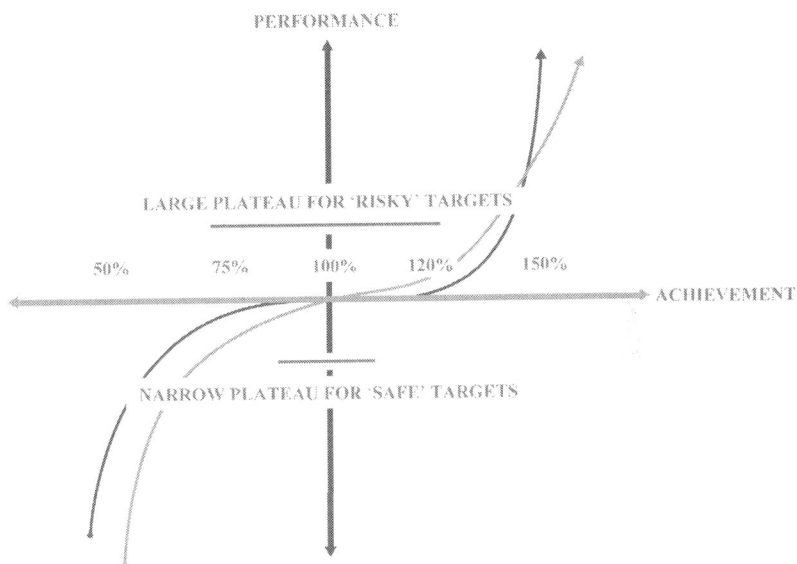

In our template, we define 5 points of achievement, but you can define more, especially on the over-achievement side to reward exceptional performers.

Results at the end of the period

During the first cycles, it is important to remember that the system is still under development. Whatever the results, whether very low or very high, we must take a lot of circumspection when leveraging this performance.

You should not blame employees who do not perform at the initial stage but rather work at building up the system accuracy and relevancy.

Alike, you should wait for a few cycles before using the roadmap as a basis to distribute bonus as risks of a setback for employees would cost them too much and would limit their acceptance. You can decide as well to apply the roadmap to only a few selected employees and introduce it as a pilot without a direct correlation with the calculation of their bonus.

6.7 The importance of coaching

We all know that each leader has a role of coach for his or her employees, but we need to know what to coach about. The roadmap and the 360° behavioral assessment create an agenda. The coaching purpose is to help each employee to develop the skills required to achieve their roadmap. To maintain attention and commitment on the roadmap and 360° behavioral assessments, it is critically important to organize several coaching sessions in the middle of the cycle. Most leaders do the mistake of forgetting the roadmap once designed and until it is time for final review. That gives a wrong message to employees that these tools are not that important for the leaders, as even themselves does not refer to it. Without strong reminders from the leaders, the employees will tend to forget their objectives and targets. By regular reminders, the leaders ensure that these tools stay at the top of mind of their team.

At the end of the cycle, it is time for assessing results. It is then a rare opportunity to remind employees the 5 elements of the leading architecture; mission, vision, strategies, culture, and performance

When I am visiting leaders and we discuss their leadership, I often asked them when is the last time that you revive your company vision, strategies and culture to your team. It is too often too long time ago. There are indeed little opportunities for a leader to discuss intimately these topics with his employees. We naturally tell these stories to new employees during the induction process at the time they are joining the company. We then consider that they know and that they are supposed to stay engaged forever. We may refresh the stories every year during a speech at an annual event but it will never have the impact of a face-to-face discussion.

The performance review (quarterly, half-year or annual) is actually the perfect opportunity to reconnect the employee performance within the leadership framework. We must imagine that they are a new employee that we want to recruit and that we want to re-engage. The leaders must prepare and structure the performance review of their direct reports with the ambition to get participants;

- Excited – again – by the team vision
- Convinced – again – by the relevancy and originality of the strategy
- Comfortable – again – about the standard behaviors
- Familiar – again – about leader's expectations
- Accurate – again – about the way his performance is measured

Experiences show that nothing lasts and regular reinforcement of the leading platforms is required. There are indeed many contradictory messages every month that could trouble the understanding from employees about leaders intentions. Frustrations are building up with difficulties and obstacles and a small inconsistency in the leaders' speeches or behaviors could lead to wrong perceptions or conclusions.

The reinforcement about the leadership platform is therefore essential to ensure sufficient understanding. Furthermore, the repetition will show to employees how important these messages are for the leaders. As we already said earlier, the frequency is more efficient than intensity to get messages across.

6.8 The benefits behind the Performance Management System

Tom Geist mentioned that execution drives the success of leaders and I personally believe that the roadmap and the 360° behavioral assessment drives the success of execution. When properly introduced in an organization within a constructive context, these tools will drive employees' accountabilities, engagement, alignment and help clarifications.

Accountabilities

As managers, we often believe that our directions have been understood and it is now up to the employees to deliver. My experiences show that failures to deliver are very often coming from a misunderstanding of expectations. Job descriptions and managers' directives are often built on actions required but do not give sufficient perspectives to employees to adjust their actions when the context is evolving.

For a proper understanding of the job, it is necessary to explain to his employee how his job is contributing to the long-term company plan and what level of deliverables we expect from him. We must give a clear picture of the landing point so that employees can correct themselves in the course of actions whatever challenges and opposition they are facing.

Leaders must understand that they do not have the same context as each of their team members. What is obvious for them is not for all their colleagues and it is their responsibilities to give their team a sufficient perspective.

Before blaming employees' abilities in executing the strategy, leaders must first question their efficiencies in giving them sufficient perspectives on the WHY behind each job and task and in clarifying expectations.

Whenever possible, the wording of the objective should match the following structure;

"Ensure that you (output expected)...so that the company can...(contribution to the organization)."

Quantify expectations

We mentioned earlier the importance of communicating accurately leader's expectations to each member of his team. The roadmap enables the leader to go one step further by quantifying the expectations. It is one thing to know that something is important; it is even more powerful to know how much. The quantification helps the employee to adjust his effort depending on the gap to the target.

You do not organize your job the same way when you are told to organize training or when you understand that you must ensure that every employee of a specific department (excluding employee left or arrived) should attend at least 2 training of more than 1 hour each on the period.

One time, I attended the preparation of the roadmap of an administrative officer working for an Asian affiliate of a Scandinavian company. The officer knew for years that it was important in that company to be compliant with the local law and avoid any penalty. During the design of the roadmap, the general manager confirms this point but he proposes to include an objective for not having any financial penalty on the period with a weight of 40% of the total performance. It was a major surprise for the administrative officer. She knew it was important but not that much important. She argued about it and managed to reduce the weight to only 20%. Such re-alignment would not have been possible if both did not have to quantify expectations and the officer would not have been so sensitive if it was not touching her own performance. From that day, she changed her behaviors and became much more cautious about legal compliance.

Support motivation

Becoming successful and being recognized by others as such is an important agenda for employees from the moment that the roadmap makes it possible. Herzberg multiplied his experiences in various countries and context and he found a similar conclusion. Success is potentially an important driver of motivation. It may not be the case today in some organizations as the leaders in place do not leverage this force yet, because the employees are not proud enough of what they are doing and because the tools in place are not objective and credible enough to emphasize individual success. The leaders are wasting the main driving energy and they, therefore, must work on their leadership architecture.

This energy may not have the same strength for everyone. As Herzberg (and Maslow) underlined, we need to solve the issues related to the hygiene factors (lower level in the Maslow pyramid) before we get access to satisfaction through the motivation factors. It is not a question of status but a question of context. Every layer of an organization can potentially be motivated by the idea of being successful.

94 | Why Should They Care?

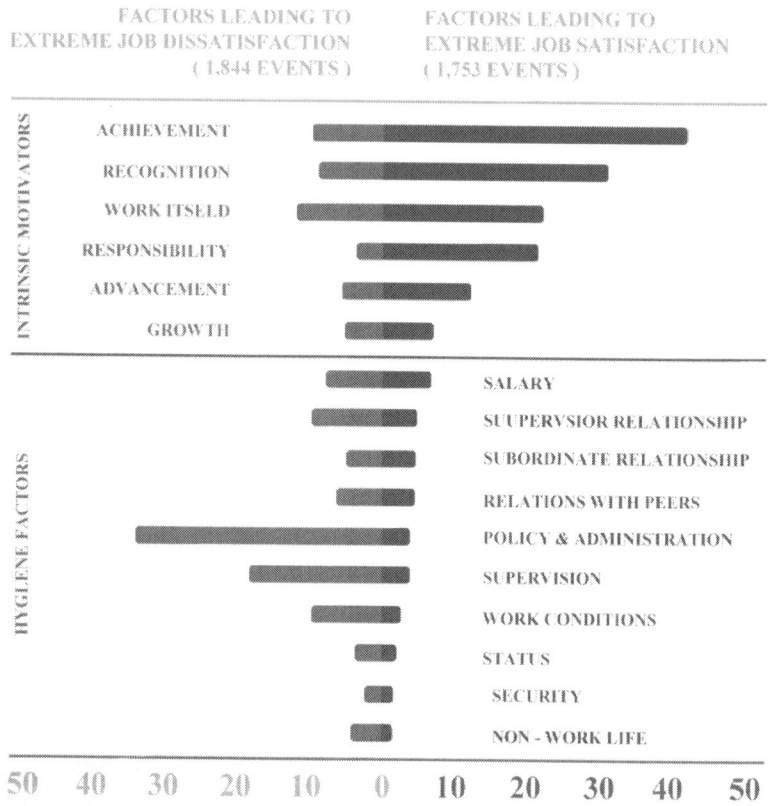

Moreover, success is a long-lasting driver and is addictive. Success is by nature associated with a project and we constantly need to keep on performing to maintain it. We are enjoying the status and it would be painful to lose it. The more successful we are, the higher is our personal equity and the more painful it is to fail. If a leader can create a culture of success in his organization, he will create a long-term competitive advantage.

Enforce alignment

We saw earlier that roadmap should include at least 30% of collective objectives that they will share with other members of their team. Having the same objective encourage you to collaborate if you want to improve your chances of success.

During my coaching of leaders, they often share with me their difficulties to get their team to collaborate. We are then going through their leadership architecture;

1. Reinforcing the common goals as mission, vision, strategies
2. Ensuring that the culture is well understood and encouraged
3. Sharing similar objectives between colleagues' roadmap (and make sure they know it)

The objectives to share must be as close as possible to their main mission in order to get their highest attention. It should actually be their closest common factor; margin value to share between sales team and marketing team, sales of new products during the first 3 years to be shared between sales and product development department, etc…

The roadmap and the 360° behavioral assessment will not only clarify expectations for employees' own job but it could actually help to understand each other's priorities. These tools are actually forging alignment in organizations. Everybody starts understanding what his or her colleagues are running after. It helps them to understand them better and to help them whenever it is possible.

By sharing these tools to employees (mainly the roadmap objectives), leaders are actually giving them common goals that they can align to. It would minimize misunderstanding and foster collaboration.

Once an employee understands that he has the same objective in their roadmap than his colleagues, he will realize that his success depends on his colleagues 'one. He will start collaborating with them, not by philanthropy but rather to maximize his roadmap results.

Google is using a similar system as the roadmap concept presented in this book. They call it OKR (Objectives and Key Results) and it has a strong influence on the way employees interact with each other. Rick Klau, Partner at YouTube explains that when an employee is preparing a meeting with colleagues and he expects them to support his proposal, he will consult each participant's OKR on Google intranet (roadmaps are indeed shared to all employees in Google) to understand what their main objectives for that period are. It is important information for him to adjust his presentation in line with his colleagues' priorities.

CONCLUSION

The common point between all the processes that we detailed in this book is predictability. Once everybody is aligned with the same vision supported by the same culture and knowing each other's priorities, we can predict how things will happen for us and for others. The roadmap gives us a clear picture about expectations and helps us anticipate our performance. It gives us visibility on our work on the period.

This comfort reassures us and allows us to organize ourselves within the space of freedom created. It is a contract of trust with our boss and our peers. As long as we contribute to the vision as specified in our roadmap and respect the behaviors detailed in the culture, our leaders will empower us in organizing our work the way that works the best for us.

Such alignment reinforces interpersonal trust. Transversal collaboration is more efficient if we can anticipate how our colleagues react to a project or an obstacle. We minimize resistances and allocate our resources more efficiently.

In a routine environment, leadership may not be critical. We are already in a comfort zone where we know what tomorrow will be about, same as today. As soon as a change is needed, leadership is required to define the new landing point, exemplifies the new behaviors, measure the progress and celebrate success. Besides predictability, leaders bring energy to an organization. Success and pride are the fuel of all human activity and it is the leader's job to create the context that will enable his team to gain such a motive.

If we look in the past at the historical faces who changed the world, they marked their time by the nature of the dreams they proposed and the exemplarity of their behaviors. They created a large community of followers who were driven by the will to contribute to the vision elaborated by their leaders and convinced about the relevance of the culture that they exhibit.

We always say that leadership emerges during difficult times. It is indeed when the present is troubled that we are more reactive to somebody who would propose us a better future and demonstrate exemplary behaviors as part of the strategy. We want to believe him as the future he describes looks much better than our difficult present.

We may not always reach the vision that we define. We may as well change sometimes the ambition and the targets that we set. The most important is to not to achieve the vision but it is to create a trajectory. At any moment, a team must be sharing common leadership architecture. A leader has for sure the possibility to adjust the architecture sometimes, but he must then quickly re-align all his team on the new one without leaving any time of uncertainties and blurriness. As soon as the architecture is not clear, individuals stop to engage. They are lacking the comfortable predictability. Why should they take the risk of investing their time and energy if they do not know whether it will contribute to their success? Why should they care if they do not get anything in exchange?

ANNEX 1

#	Examples of objectives
1	Ensure that company reaches its budgeted 3rd party net sales (after customer discount and rebates and excluding intra-company gross
2	Ensure that customer cash discount do not exceed the percentage of gross sales as indicated in target 0
3	Ensure that the monthly average receivables ratio stays below target 0 (target expressed in days of net sales - sum of every month ratio /
4	Ensure that Customer A grow by target
5	Ensure that new customer (initiated in 2011) reaches the annual sales contribution of target
6	Ensure that the average order size exceeds target
7	Ensure that the number of salesmen below target do not exceed target
8	Ensure that the number of SKU (to be qualified a SKU should be higher than x millions of annual net sales) exceeding 50% GP exceeds
9	Ensure that the weighted gross price average increases as target
10	Ensure that the number of products lower than 50 millions of annual gross sales do not exceed target
11	Ensure that the Product A or Range B reaches the GP% as target
12	Ensure that the average net sales of the new product (launched after Jan 1st, 2008) reaches the amount indicated as target
13	Ensure that the new product (launched after Jan 1st, 2011) reaches the contribution indicated as target
14	Ensure that gross profit (according to management report) stays above the level of target
15	Ensure that Product A grow as target
16	Ensure that number of products below 0.05% of gross profit value (excluding products launched in the year) do not exceed target
17	Ensure that the number of seminars (included only seminars included more than x customers) organized in the period exceeds target
18	Ensure that the document X is prepared before date indicated as target
19	Formally provide at least 3 major additional ideas of Continuous Improvement and ensure that all these ideas are implemented before
20	Ensure that the expenses do not exceed target
21	Ensure that the investment does not exceed target
22	Ensure that the EBIT % reaches target
23	Ensure that the GMP certificate is renewed before target
24	Ensure that the manufacturing indirect and labour expenses variance stays positive
25	Ensure that annual average of the monthly backorders value do not exceed target
26	Ensure that the average manufacturing delays (difference between first confirmed date of manufacturing and date of release) do not
27	Ensure that the weighted average purchase price of the 5 raw materials indicated in the sheet attached increase not more than target
28	Ensure that the purchase from supplier A reaches the % of total purchase as indicated in target 0
29	Ensure that production plan or purchase plan (or any other plan or report) are sent before date indicated as target
30	Ensure that stock differences (addition of absolute value) along the year do not exceed the value indicated as target
31	Ensure that production line stoppage because of breakdown do not exceed the limit as target
32	Ensure that every raw materials reception are processed (stored and entered in ERP system) within leadtime indicated as target
33	Ensure that credit claims for delivery mistake do not exceed the limit (value in % of gross sales) indicated as target
34	Ensure that the monthly average stock ratio of Product A or Range B stays below target (target expressed in days of COGS - sum of every month ratio / 12)
35	Ensure that the average delivery leadtime (between order reception and product delivery date) do not exceed target
36	Ensure that all QC reactives carries an expiry date
37	Ensure that the average leadtime of analysis do not exceed target
38	Ensure that the Y3 estimated sales potential of the products in development (PID) exceeds the amount mentioned as target (to be counted as PID, a project must be validated by Mr X)
39	Ensure that you obtain the registration of the product A (based on the date of the certificate) before target
40	Organize at least 3 finance training for all our department managers. The agenda must be proposed at least 2 weeks before the meeting
41	Ensure that the position A recruitment is finalized (contract signed) before target
42	Ensure that the number of road maps implemented exceed target
43	Ensure that the expenses of training exceeds the percentage of gross sales (or gross profit) mentioned in target
44	Ensure that audit report is finalized before target
45	Ensure that budget is validated before target
46	Ensure that the difference between full year net profit value estimated in september and the audited annual net profit value do not exceed
47	Ensure that ROIC (EBIT /(Assets - payables)) exceed target
48	Ensure that the company reach the budgeted EBIT value
49	Ensure that employee severance provisions are correctly provisionned from Q1
50	Ensure that the company generates a minimum of cash as indicated in target (Cash = EBITDA - working capital variation - CAPEX)

ANNEX 2 – KPISOFT.COM

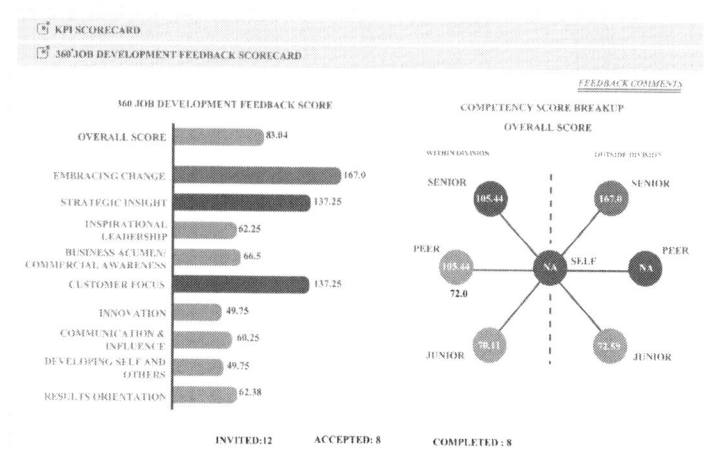

ANNEX 3

INDIVIDUAL ROADMAP
Q4 2013

Name:
Title:
Company:

#	Individual objectives	Target 50%	Target 75%	Target 100%	Target 120%	Target 150%	Deadline	Weight	Achievements / Comments	Performance	Results
1	Ensure that the company reaches its targeted third party net sales (after customer discount and rebates and excluding intra-company gross sales)	40	42	44	49	52	31-Aug-18	20%	Third party's net sales reached 54 millions	150%	30.00%
2	Ensure that the intra-company purchase reaches the target in % of total net sales	10%	11%	14%	18%	19%	31-Aug-18	5%	The intra-company purchase represented 18% of the total net sales	100%	5.00%
3	Ensure that the company reach the targeted EBIT value (including intra-company activity)	8	8.2	8.7	9.3	12.3	31-Aug-18	25%	EBIT = 8.8	100%	25.00%
4	Ensure that the monthly average stock ratio (RM+PK+FP) stays below target's targets expressed in days of COGS - sum of every month ratio / 12)	160	142	120	110	105	31-Aug-18	10%	Average monthly stock ratio on the period = 145 days of COGS	50%	5.00%
5	Ensure that the monthly average receivables ratio stays below targets (targets expressed in days of net sales - sum of every month ratio / 12)	35	32	25	23	22	31-Aug-18	5%	Average monthly receivables ratio on the period = 23 days of net sales	120%	6.00%
6	Ensure that gross margin (according to management report) stays above the level of targets	34%	34.80%	36.30%	37.50%	38.30%	31-Aug-18	10%	Gross margin = 33.8%	0%	0.00%
7	Ensure that customers segment A (cf attached file) reach the annual sales contribution as targets	32%	35%	40%	42%	43%	31-Aug-18	5%	The customer A contribution represented 42% of the sales	75%	3.75%
8	Ensure that the 10 products listed in the annex grow as targeted compared to 2017 sales	16%	18%	20%	23%	24%	31-Aug-18	10%	The average gross sales growth on the period for the 10 products listed in the annex was 25%	150%	15.00%
9	Ensure that clear roadmaps are implemented to all your direct report within the validation of your superior within the targeted agenda	25-Aug	20-Aug	15-Aug	05-Aug	31-Jul	31-Jul	1%	Roadmaps have been implemented to all direct report before August 3rd	150%	1.5%
							Total	**140%**		**Total**	**105%**

Comments:
The overall Roadmap performance on that period reached 105% thanks to an outstanding performance for the objective 1, 5, 8 and 9

Signature employee   **Signature supervisor**

Printed in Poland
by Amazon Fulfillment
Poland Sp. z o.o., Wrocław